# Captain Psychology's
## How to Learn Vocabulary:
## Psychology of Learning

Dr. Ken Tangen

ISBN-10:0-9765360-4-8
ISBN-13:978-0976536048

# DEDICATION

To my students, who always teach me so much.

DEDICATION

To the memory of ...

# CONTENTS

# ACKNOWLEDGMENTS

The terms are common to the areas of education and psychology. But the definitions, misinterpretations, oversights and errors are mine alone. Thanks to all who reviewed early drafts of the manuscript and added their valuable insights. Special thanks to Katrina Tangen for her keen editorial eye.

# Part I

# PART 1: START HERE

I introduced the OPT-Repeat model for learning vocabulary in *Captain Psychology's How to Learn Vocabulary: Biological Psychology*. In this four step model, OPT means to organize, process and test. Repeat means that the process is recursive. You often have to go through the organize-process-test steps repeatedly.

You can use this model for learning any list of terms, as I'll demonstrate is this book by using terms about the psychology of learning. University courses on learning are often called behavioral change, learning theories or simply learning. We will focus on learning terms from a typical psychology course about learning, but the steps will work on any list.

In Part 1, we will start with 101 terms from the psychology of learning. I've created the list for you. We are going to master this material using the OPT-Repeat model.

In Part 2, we will add an additional 900 terms about the principles of learning. We will tackle the whole list of 1001 items, using the same OPT-Repeat model.

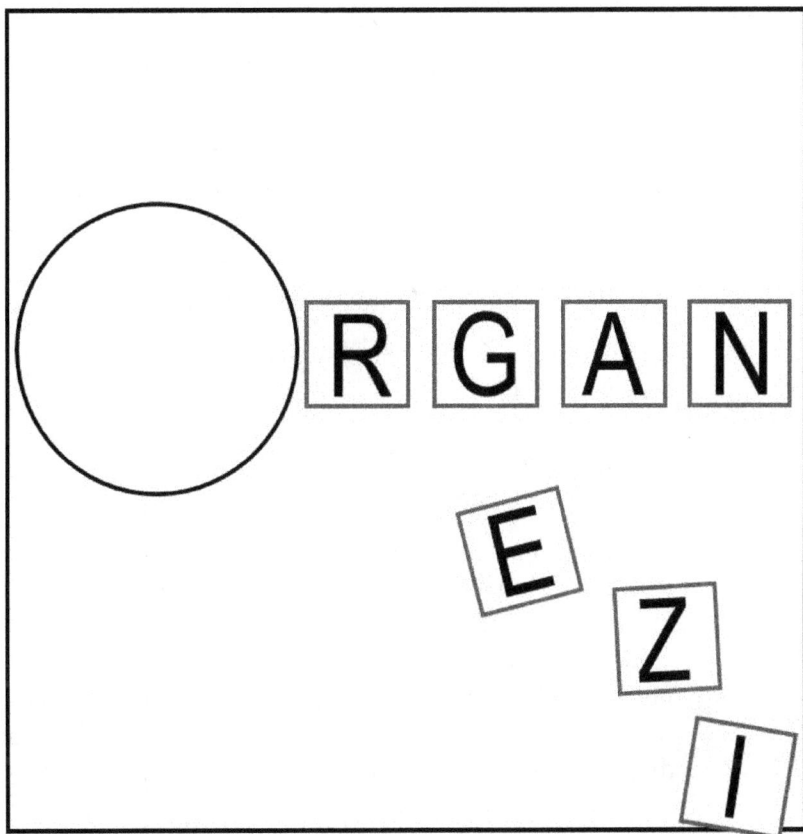

# ORGANIZE

Facts require organization. It is difficult to remember individual facts. It is better when the facts are grouped into meaningful units. It is best when our meaningful units are small.

Lists, then, are good news and bad news. The good news about lists is that they are not individual items. The terms have been organized into a list. There is a structure to it, or structure can be given to it. And there are several structures to chose from (alphabetical, conceptual, time line, etc.).

The bad news is that lists usually are not well organized and they are too long.

## Organization

In general, an alphabetical list is not a well organized list. It is a form of organization, and it is better than no organization at all, but alphabetical lists have two main purposes. First, they allow you to easily check for duplicates. If you want to make sure there are no duplications in the list, sort the items into an alphabetical list. Second, alphabetical lists are great for looking things up. Alphabetical lists are perfect for dictionaries, glossaries and packing lists. It is a simple structure that is easy to access.

For learning, alphabetical lists lack meaning. The more meaningful structure the better. We want our lists to be clustered or categorized. We want lists with lots of structure.

## Length

For learning, lists tend to be too long. If you're given one long list of terms, you need to break it down into smaller segments. Learn a bit at a time. Don't try to swallow it whole.

As long as people have had lists, we've known that shorter is better. You know this from your own experience. If given a choice between to lists of equal difficulty, you would select the shortest of them. Research proves it is true. Short lists are easy and long lists are hard.

The longer the list, the harder it is to remember the middle. We remember the first part and the last part of a long list but we forget the items in the middle. This phenomenon is called the serial position effect. It occurs because we have two memory systems at work when we're learning a list. Working memory helps us remember the last items in a list because we haven't dumped them out yet. We are still "working" on them. We remember the first part of a list because we've stored it in long-term memory. It is not consolidated or permanent but is in the temporary store of long-term memory. At night, we move items from temporary long-term memory to a sparsely-encoded consolidated more permanent memory. We have no memory system devoted to recalling items in the middle of a list.

## An Obvious Solution

The obvious solution is to divide long lists into shorter ones.

# 101 Terms

I believe there are only three things you can learn: facts, concepts and behaviors. So, I've created a list of 101 terms about facts. We will look at concepts and behaviors later. Focusing only on facts is another way of dividing and conquering.

I took all the names out of the list. There are only two techniques named for theorists and one note taking system named for a college. By removing them there is more structure.

Here is what to do.

# 1. Make A List of Don't-Knows

An odd aspect of our memory systems is that we can immediately tell if we don't know something. This is called negative recognition. You know you've never heard the word "Smiwpook." I know you've never heard it because I just made it up. But it isn't clear why you know for certain that you don't know it.

It is reasonable to assume that you would have to search your memory banks for all strange works you've heard, or all words that start with S. But you don't have to conduct a search. It is not clear why our memories work that way but let's use it to your advantage.

I'll give you a list of words. Scan them quickly. Mark it if you don't know it, and move on. Negative recognition is a fast and accurate way of identifying a sublist: a group of words and phrases you don't know.

Mark it as a Don't-Know if it is a single word you don't know. Mark it if it is a phrase you don't know, even if you know the individual words.

Here is a list of 101 things relating to facts, as opposed to concepts or behaviors.

Ready?

Scan!

**Alphabetical List of 101 Terms About Facts**

30 days hath September, April, June
ABCDEFG song
acronym
acrostic
adjacent associations
alphabet-concrete image pegs
alphabet-rhyme pegs
associated pairs
avoid flow
backward chaining
blocking
categories
chunking
clustering
color, size, shape, bold, underlying
competence
complete memory
contextual distinctiveness
Cornell note-taking system
CVCs
distinctiveness
don't forget
doodling
egg and spear technique
elaboration mnemonics
emotional distinctiveness
encoding specificity principle
expanded retrieval strategy
external mnemonics
flashcards
flow
forward chaining
how to learn lists
infographic
interactive images
item familiarity
item similarity
journey method

link & story systems
list length
LMNOP
location cues
meaningful
memory palace
method of loci
mind map
mnemonics
naieve mnemonics
negative recognition
nicknames
nonsense words
note taking
number-rhyme reversal system
number-rhyme system
order of presentation
outline
overlearning
peg systems
personal experience
photographs
positive recognition
primacy
primary distinctiveness
RADAR
RDO
recency
reduction mnemonics
rehearsal
repetition
retrieve often
review
rewrite your notes
rhymes
same order every time
savings
secondary distinctiveness
sentence completion

serial interleaving
serial position effect
serial recall
state-dependent learning
storyboard
string on your finger
structural overview
study skills
switch tasks
teach someone
technical mnemonics
test self
total time hypothesis
translation schemes
two as a swan
unidirectional bonds
visualization
vividness
von Restorff Effect
within list associations
word association
word-completion items
write it down
Zeigarnik Effect


Making a list of Don't-Knows should be the first step in learning any list. It makes a smaller list, and gives you a place to start. Before we look up the definitions to our Don't-Knows, let's make a couple of other lists.

## 2. Make A List of Things Likely to Be on The Test

Make a list of things you think will be on the test. How do you know what to study? Use my Rule of Three. A word or phrase is likely to be on the test if:

- it is mentioned in class

- it is in the class notes

- it is in the textbook

If it is in all three, study it hard. If it is only two, study it medium. If it is only in one, give it a little study, just in case.

Scan through the master list again and identify your Test-Likelys.

# 3. Make A List by Categories

Make a series of lists, one for each major category of information. You get to choose the categories but easy choice is by theorists, time eras and by application (clinical, research or theoretical, for example).

There are no theorists in our current list, at least not enough to make a category. But keep it in mind when we get to our lists of 1001 terms.

Similarly, time eras and application categories aren't particularly helpful with this list but that's the point. Try lot of different categories and use what works.

For variety, try arbitrarily selecting a group of terms, by a beginning letter, for example. Here are the words that start with R:

RADAR
RDO
recency
reduction mnemonics
rehearsal
repetition
retrieve often
review
rewrite your notes
rhymes

As you look through the list, you'll find that this group of terms is pretty well distributed across the alphabet. There isn't an overwhelming number of terms that begin with any particular letter. It was worth a try because every data set is different. If we had found most of the terms start with the letter S, we could then subdivide that category into small segments.

You can create as many sub-lists as you wish. I came up with nine See what you think.

The first is about mnemonics:
  Mnemonics
  Naïve mnemonics
      rhymes
          30 days hath September, April, June
          ABCDEFG song
      chunking
          LMNOP
      forward chaining
      nicknames
      rehearsal
  Technical mnemonics
      acronym
          RADAR
          RDO
      acrostic
      backward chaining
      blocking
      categories
      clustering
      link & story systems
      memory palace
          method of loci
          journey method
      peg systems
          alphabet-concrete image pegs
          alphabet-rhyme pegs
      translation schemes
          two as a swan
          egg and spear technique
      number-rhyme reversal system
      number-rhyme system
  External mnemonics
      string on your finger
      write it down
  Reduction mnemonics
  Elaboration mnemonics

List 2 is about memory:
Memory
 recency
 primacy
 serial interleaving
 serial recall
 state-dependent learning


List 3 is about Ebbinghaus:
Ebbinghaus
 adjacent associations
 complete memory
 CVCs
 nonsense words
 savings
 serial position effect
 how to learn lists
 total time hypothesis
 within list associations


Lists 4 is about the research of Mary Calkins:
Calkins
 associated pairs
 sentence completion
 vividness
 unidirectional bonds
 word association
 word-completion items


List 5 is about distinctiveness:
Distinctiveness
 color, size, shape, bold, underlying
 primary distinctiveness
  von Restorff Effect
  contextual distinctiveness
 secondary distinctiveness

emotional distinctiveness
Zeigarnik Effect

Lists 6-9 are based on OPT-Repeat
    Organize
        encoding specificity principle
        item familiarity
        item similarity
        list length
        location cues
        meaningful
        positive recognition
        negative recognition
        order of presentation
        study skills
        note taking
          outline
          Cornell note-taking system
        personal experience

    Process
        Verbally
        Visually
         infographic
         interactive images
         mind map
         doodling
         storyboard
         structural overview
         visualization

Test
> expanded retrieval strategy
> don't forget
> flashcards
> flow
> test self
> switch tasks
> teach someone
> competence
> avoid flow
> review
> photographs

Repeat
> overlearning
> repetition
> retrieve often
> rewrite your notes
> same order every time

# 4. Make A List of Personal Interests

There are two goals to taking a class: getting through it and getting something out of it. These are not mutually exclusive goals but they are not identical. I took classes that impacted me greatly but I didn't ace. And I've taken classes where my grades were great but the class was a waste of time.

Do both. Study to get through the class. And identify something in the class material that you can take with you. There is no reason you can't improve your life while you get through school. You can do both.

Look for at least one thing that is helpful or interesting to you. If you can find one good idea in every chapter and every lecture, you'll have a great head start in improving your own life. While you're looking at this material, don't forget to add items to your "Someday When I Feel Like It" list.

# PROCESS

# PROCESS

Lists are good, and short lists are best, but regardless of their length, you must process them. Don't leave them in their original state. Elaborate them. Here's how to start.

First, look up all of the terms on your Don't-Know list. Second, process the information verbally, using your semantic memory. Third, process the information graphically, using your visuospatial memory.

Let's take a look at each in some detail.

# 1. Look Up Don't-Knows

It's time to do something with the lists you've made. A good place to begin is to look up the definitions of your Don't-Knows. They were easy to identify and you'll make quick progress. Tackling your Don't-Knows will give you the biggest bang for your buck. It doesn't take long to convert Don't-Knows to Sort-of-Knows.

Here are the definitions for the terms about Facts:

# Definitions of Terms About Facts

**30 days hath September, April, June…** A rhyming mnemonic. An effective naïve mnemonic.

**ABCDEFG song**. An example of forward chaining. We learn the first part of the song best; worse as you get to middle.

**acronym**. A reduction mnemonic which shortens a series of words into a series of letters. American Broadcasting Company becomes ABC. Regular Day Off becomes RDO. Radio Detection And Ranging becomes RADAR (RAdio Detection And Ranging). Unlike acrostics, the letter must stay in the same order.

**acrostic**. A reduction mnemonic which creates a new word out of the initial letters of a group of words. The order of the letters can be changed to optimize its effectiveness. The personality dimensions for the Big Five can be CANOE or OCEAN, whichever is preferred. Helpful for remember the number and order of items. Not helpful for remembering the desired underlying terms.

**adjacent associations**. For Ebbinghaus, items that have associations with other items on a list are easier to learn. List with items close or next to each other (adjacent) are even easier to learn.

**alphabet-concrete image pegs**. A technical mnemonic technique that uses concrete images that start with the same letter. A is ape or apple, b is boy, c is cat or cot or car, etc.

**alphabet-rhyme pegs**. A technical mnemonic technique used to spell words. Pegs are based on sound-alikes. A is hay or ale. B is bee. C is see. Not as widely used as concrete image pegs because some rhymes are difficult to create.

**associated pairs**. Paired associates were first studied by Mary Whiton Calkins. Use pairs of words, she showed that the greatest influence on memory was number of presentations, followed by vividness, followed by recency. Her research led Jung and others to use word associations.

**avoid flow**. When you are using interleafed practice, the sensation of flow (everything going easily) is a signal to change to another learning activity.

**backward chaining**. An effective mnemonic for learning speeches, songs and long passages text. Also used to train dogs and teach children with developmental issues how to dress themselves. Begin the with last item you want performed, then add to the beginning of the chain. The 12 Days of Christmas is a good example.

**blocking**. Putting similar items together. TV news shows put all the sports stories together in a block. Similarly, they block the weather stories, traffic reports and kitten videos.

**categories**. Grouping of words or ideas by similarity. Recalling using categories is easier than not, even if no categories were provided to you.

**chunking**. The naïve mnemonic of breaking a long sequence into smaller segments. Shown in our perceptual system by items close together being groups together. Chunks contain 3-4 items or 3-4 chunks of items.

**clustering**. Both informal (put similar items together) and formal multivariate cluster analysis are used to identify commonality between ideas.

**color, size, shape, bold, underlying**…. Variations that make text more memorable.

**competence**. Confidence proceeds competence. We become competent (able to perform a skill) after we are confident we can do it. We must practice beyond confidence.

**complete memory**. Ebbinghaus' term for remembering a list completely one time.

**contextual distinctiveness**. Also called primary distinctiveness. One aspect stands out compared to the context. The von Restroff effect is the result of printing a word in a different color in the middle of a list; make the word easier to remember and makes the whole list easier to remember.

**Cornell note-taking system**. Notes are taken in the main section (right 2/3$^{rd}$ of a page) in outline form. Afterwards, or when it pops into your head, questions are put in the left 1/3$^{rd}$ section of the page. At the bottom of the page (or the end of the notes), a paraphrase summary of the important ideas is written. This system is particularly helpful as a reminder that processing your notes is as important as taking them.

**CVCs**. Consonant-vowel-consonant combinations used to make artificial words for studying memory. Used to learn lists, like Ebbinghaus.

**distinctiveness**. A process of focusing attention. Three major types: primary (von Restroff), secondary (1$^{st}$ time experiences) and emotional (Zeigarnik effect).

**don't forget**. Tangen's general principle that it is easier to keep things in memory than to put them there. Check periodically to see if what you've learned is still there. Use the expanded rehearsal strategy.

**doodling**. Random drawings can aid learning by focusing your attention on your notes while you listen to a lecture.

**egg and spear technique**. A number-shape mnemonic system, representing each number with a distinctive shape.

**elaboration mnemonics**. Adding something to make it easier to remember. Includes storytelling and sentence formation. Every Good Boy Does Fine is an elaboration mnemonic for remembering the lines of a treble clef (EGBDF).

**emotional distinctiveness**. The impact happy emotions have on memory. Generally, the addition of emotion and cognition.

**encoding specificity principle**. Training is best when the conditions of learning match the conditions of performance.

**expanded retrieval strategy**. Also called the expanded rehearsal strategy. Lengthen or shorten retrieval sessions based on the accessibility of memories.

**external mnemonics**. Writing things down, getting them out of your head. Timers, diaries, journals, calendars, etc.

**flashcards**. Originally, a card with a small amount of information held up by a teacher as a learning aid for students. More commonly, a study aid created by students for themselves. A cue or prompt is written on one side of a card. The other side of the card contains the definition or response to the cue.

**flow**. Once of Seligman's definitions of happiness; a steady stream of meditation calm, usually from repeated action. In studying, an indication to switch to another topic.

**forward chaining**. Serial learning. Links are added to the end of the chain. The typical way of learning a song. A naïve mnemonic.

**how to learn lists**. Confirmed by Ebbinghaus, the best way to learn lists is repetition.

**infographic**. A combination of information and graphic. A graphic summary of the steps of a process or the main points covered in a lesson. Isotypes and international symbols are examples of simple infographics.

**interactive images**. The key to remembering images is to make them interactive. In technical mnemonics, users of peg systems are often told to visualize weird images. This works only because interactive images are often weird.

**item familiarity**. Items in a list which are familiar to us are easier to remember.

**item similarity**. Items in a list which are similar to each other are easier to remember.

**journey method**. Another name of the method of loci. You "journey" your way from place to place, remembering one item at each stop.

**link & story systems**. Technical mnemonic techniques. Links are created by putting the words you want to remember into a chain or flow chart. Story mnemonics put the words or tasks you want to remember into a story (the car needs new brakes but want to stop by the bakery first).

**list length**. Confirmed by Ebbinghaus, the longer a list, the more difficult it is to learn. A natural outgrowth of this principle is to divide long lists into small lists.

**LMNOP**. When children learn the alphabet, they learn these letters as a single word or chunk.

**location cues**. When we form a memory, we also record meta data. We extract the meaning of a situation, file away the elements needed to recreate the memory, and encode where we are and who we are with. These location cues help you remember in the kitchen but forget in the living room, and then remember again when in the kitchen.

**meaningful**. In general, we remember things that are meaningful to us. Chunking is a naïve mnemonic technique which creates meaningful units of information. Self-association with our experiences make some information easier to remember (e.g., your birth year in a series of numbers).

**memory palace**. A technical mnemonic stategory for placing images in loctions. The palace can be a remembered real place or an imagined one. Sherlock Holms' use of the method of loci. Each room in the palace has objects, and each object is associated with a piece of information.

**method of loci**. A technical mnemonic strategy used by ancients Greeks and Romans. Combines images and places. Places (loci) are used as anchors or pegs. At each place, you store an image of what you want to remember. Information must be converted into images. Playing cards would be converted into images of famous people or people you know.

**mind map**. A version of a concept map. A single work is written in the middle of a page and other words, thoughts, pictures and information is linked to it. A visual guide to understanding a field of knowledge.

**mnemonics**. Techniques for remembering better. Classified as naïve (done naturally) or technical (taught).

**naieve mnemonics**. Memory techniques people do automatically, without training. These include repretition, singing-rhymer, chunking and forward chaining.

**negative recognition**. Immediate knowledge that you don't know something. Don't have to search for the meaning of the word Ksuqoopf; immediately know you've never heard or seen it. Unclear how we know they without an exhaustive search.

**nicknames**. A naïve mnemonic technique. We tend to shorten people's names and titles to something easier to remember.

**nonsense words**. Originally used by Ebbinghaus. Typically, consonant-vowel-consonant combinations.

**note taking**. An external mnemonic technique. We write down what we want to study later. Most learning comes from reviewing and rewriting notes.

**number-rhyme reversal system**. A technical mnemonic technique. Numerical pegs (1, 2, 3) are visualized as objects that rhyme (sun, shoe, tree). In order to remember numbers, compound images are formed (sun-tree-tree-shoe would be 1331).

**number-rhyme system**. A technical mnemonic; a type of peg system. The pegs are rhymes for numbers. Instead of 1-2-3, you use sun, shoe and tree. For each peg, you visualize an item. If you want to buy bread, milk and socks, you visualize the sun eating bread, milk in a shoe (or a cow in a shoe), and a tree of socks.

**order of presentation**. Serial learning doesn't allow items to be rearranged into more meaningful units. If order of presentation is up to you, items can be arranged at will. Most important thing first takes advantage of primacy. Most important thing last takes advantage of recency.

**outline**. A tree-like structure for organizing thoughts. Main points are followed by indented sub-points, which are followed by further indented sub-sub-points. A common way to take notes.

**overlearning**. Memory increases with repetitive trials. For Ebbinghaus, continuing to study after a list has been learned error free.

**peg systems**. Technical mnemonics which are versatile but require time and effort to set up. Pegs are like kindergarten coat racks: one item per peg. The pegs can be reused. Includes number-rhyme, number-shape, alphabet rhyme, alphabet-concrete image systems.

**personal experience**. Items in a list which relate to our personal experience are easier to remember. A sequence of random number which includes your year of birth will be easier to remember.

**photographs**. An excellent external mnemonic tool for remembering your childhood.

**positive recognition**. The end of search. Recognition that you have found what you were looking for. No immediate result is guaranteed.

**primacy**. The tendency to remember the first things on a list, assuming serial recall.

**primary distinctiveness**. Context impacts recall. The von Restroff effect (colored word in middle of list).

**RADAR**. An acronym of radio detection and ranging.

**RDO**. A typical acronym for regular day off.

**recency**. The tendency in free recall to remember the most recent items.

**reduction mnemonics**. Mnemonic techniques to reduce the amount of information to be recalled, such as acronyms and nicknames.

**rehearsal**. Put everything together; repetition Naïve mnemonic of repeating a word or phrase to keep it in memory.

**repetition**. Doing something over and over. Sometimes called rehearsal.

**retrieve often**. A study technique. Retrieving material from long-term memory is better than having another encoding trial. The more information is retrieved, the more accessible it is.

**review**. Going over previous events or knowledge. For studying, consolidating and rewriting notes makes a good review.

**rewrite your notes**. Based on the idea that restructuring material improves your memory of it. Related to but not the same as Craik & Lockhart's level of processing theory.

**rhymes**. An effective naïve mnemonic. I before E...

**same order every time**. Retrieval is best when encoding trials present items in the same order every time.

**savings**. For Ebbinghaus, the number of time needed to relearn a list.

**secondary distinctiveness**. The first you do or see something.

**sentence completion**. Based on the word association studies of Mary Calkins. A tool for creativity, brainstorming and initiating conversations.

**serial interleaving**. Study A, then B, then C, then A, B, C...

**serial position effect**. In long lists of words, when asked to remember them in order, we remember the first of the list best, the end next best and the middle least well.

**serial recall**. Retrieve items in the order presented.

**state-dependent learning**. Internal states (mood, pain, etc.) impact our ability to learn and remember. When you are happy, you remember happy things. When you are sad, you remember sad things. It is easier to remember when internal states match between learning and retrieval.

**storyboard**. A graphic way to organize and sequence stories and presentations. Widely used in the production of animations, movies and video games. Originally developed in the 1930s by Walt Disney.

**string on your finger**. A physical reminder. Helps alert you that something needs to be remembered but doesn't help indicate what it is that needs to be recalled.

**structural overview**. A summary, usually visual, of what is or will be learned in a lesson. Can be used as an introduction, a review or both.

**study skills**. A series of tasks and practices used by good students. The list usually includes a designated study space, a consistent environment, note taking techniques and mnemonic strategies.

**switch tasks**. A study technique. Change to studying a different topic as proactive interference builds up. Switch on the basis of time (every 15-20 minutes) or fatigue (focus is shifting) or flow (flow is an indication you've mastered the material).

**teach someone**. A technique to improve encoding. When you are confident you understand a concept, explain it to someone else. Teaching others shows hole in our reasoning.

**technical mnemonics**. Memory techniques that don't come naturally to us but can be learned. The most helpful are method of loci (visualizing a concept at each point along a journey) and backward chaining (adding links to the front of a chain).

**test self**. A study technique. Before you take a test prepared by someone else, make up test questions and see how you would answer them.

**total time hypothesis**. Ebbinghaus proposal that recall in linearly related to how much time you spent on it.

**translation schemes**. A technical mnemonic used to remember numbers. An adaptation of the number-shape peg system. Numbers are converted into words, where digits (0 through 9) are consonants and vowels don't count. $1 = t$ (one vertical stroke), $2 = n$ (two lines), and $3 = m$ (3 vertical lines). Converts 13 into tim or tom or team (your coice).

**two as a swan**. A technical mnemonic for remembering numbers. Both a 2 and a swan have curved necks.

**unidirectional bonds**. In paired associates, bonds between words are formed in one direction. A good practice is to learn flash cards in both cue-definition and definition-cue orientations.

**visualization**. Creating and using a mental image.

**vividness**. Vivid images are easier to remember than dull images. But vividness is less important than the number of presentations, and the interactivity of mental images.

**von Restorff Effect**. A type of primary distinctiveness. A word of a different font or color in the middle of list makes the whole list easier to remember.

**within list associations**. Ebbinghaus showed that associated words within a list make the list easier to remember. If "cow" and "moo" are in the list, the normal association between them makes them easier to remember. Adjacent associations (cow and moo next to each other) are the strongest word associations.

**word association**. Words connected by shape, sound, adjacency on a list are easier to remember than words that have no associations.

**word-completion items**. An application of word-associations. Therapists and research use this task (finish the rest of the word) to indicate conflict or to test memory.

**write it down**. The advice of memory experts. Although technical mnemonics can be used, for most daily situations it is far easier to write things down.

**Zeigarnik Effect**. Named for Bluma Zeigarnik. Incomplete tasks are easier to remember than completed tasks. You can remember the plot when you are reading a chapter a day. But finish the book and the whole plot is less clear.


Remember to mark off the items from your Don't Know list when you understand them. Check off all the items you have now mastered.

## 2. Write A Story

People are great storytellers. It is how we make sense of our world. Our right hemisphere looks at the overall experience but our left hemisphere makes a logical story out of it. Here is a story using our target words. I'm sure your stories will be better. But here is an example to get you started.

Learning facts is mostly a matter of **repetition**. This is the secret of **how to learn lists**. But there are a number of **mnemonics** that can help. The best one, in my experience, it called **chunking**. It is a **naïve mnemonic**, meaning that people do it naturally, without thinking about it. I'm sure when I was little I thoguht the alphabet included **LMNOP** as a single chunk. It took me awhile to figure out that they were individual letters. Chunking occurs pretty automatically, **clustering** is thoughtfully putting things into **blocks** or **categories**, which requires more work.

I also like making up songs and **rhymes**. Remember **30 days hath September** or the **alphabet song** (ABCDEFG, won't you sing along with me)? There is something about singing your way through a test that appeals to me. It works great for listing questions.

I've tried **acronyms** (ABC instead of American Broadcasting Company, and **RDO** instead of regular day off) and **acrostics** (**RADAR** or HOMES for remember the Great Lakes), but I would remember the **nickname** or abbreviation but not what the letters stood for.

Ebbinghaus showed us that **within-list associations** make things easier to remember, and that **adjacent associations** are particularly helpful. I think his concept of **savings** and his **total time hypothesis** make sense. It's remarkable what he was able to do with **nonsense words** and **CVCs** (consonant-vowel-consonant pseudo-words). I follow his advice to go beyond **complete memory** by **overlearning**, interleaving (either **serial** or random), and distributing my practice over several days. The **serial position effect** may have been known before Ebbinghaus but the work on **primacy** and **recency** memory systems is quite recent.

When I'm required to learn a list for **serial recall** (items in order), I do it grudgingly. I prefer to change the **order of presentation** so I can arrange items into patterns that are more **meaningful** to me and to my **personal experience**. But it required, I keep the **list length** short, look for items that are **similar**, practice the items in the **same order every time**. I sometimes use **forward chaining** but I've found that **backward chaining** works so much better.

I sort of get the **number-rhyme peg system** (sun, shoe, tree) but of the **peg systems** seem like too much work to me. I can't imagine using the **number-rhyme reversal system**, the **alphabet-concrete image pegs** or the **alphabet-rhyme pegs**. I'm also not a fan of the **egg and spear technique**.

the **journey method**. It is a **technical mnemonic**, meaning that someone has taught you to use it. It is also called the **memory palace** or **method of loci**. It works by creating mental **location cues**.

I'm a visual person, so I love **mind maps, structural overviews, infographics, storyboards, doodling** and even **outlines**. I **visualize** how terms go together and create **interactive images**. The advantage of interactive images is that they tend to be **vivid** and concrete.

My **study skills** are pretty well established. A lot of what I learn comes for **teaching someone else**. I do **review, retrieve often** and **rewrite my notes** a lot. But mostly, I use **external mnemonics** such as **writing things down**, though I've never actually ever tied a **string on my finger**. I work hard at **avoiding flow**, and **switch to another task** when things feel like they are coming easily (**flow**). I **test myself** to make sure I **don't forget** what I've learned. I make my own **flashcards**, check for **competence**, and use an **expanded retrieval strategy**. Since **word associations** are

**unidirectional**, I turn my flashcards over and study them that way too.

I've never tried the **Cornel note-taking system** of dividing the page into three parts but I do most of my note taking drawing on art pads. Sometimes I write out my impressions of a group of words, like I'm doing now. It is a sort of **link & story system** taken to an extreme.


What story can you tell? See what you can do with these terms:

**associated pairs**
**color, size, shape, bold, underlying**
**contextual distinctiveness**
**distinctiveness**
**elaboration mnemonics**
**emotional distinctiveness**
**encoding specificity principle**
**item familiarity**
**negative recognition**
**photographs**
**positive recognition**
**primary distinctiveness**
**reduction mnemonics**
**rehearsal**
**secondary distinctiveness**
**sentence completion**
**state-dependent learning**
**translation schemes**
**two as a swan**
**von Restorff Effect**
**word-completion items**
**Zeigarnik Effect**

# 3. Draw A Picture

People are great at words. But we are also great at pictures. We used words in Write a Story, let's switch to pictures. Let's draw a picture.

Some people believe that pictures are more symbolic, thus easier to remember. Part of this is certainly true. Allan Paivio's research on remembering lists of images shows that they are easier to remember than lists of words. The idea has its flaws (concrete pictures are easier to remember than abstract words but abstract pictures don't seem to be that memorable or distinctive. Still, there is no reason not to try being more visual.

## Clusters

Put a term or phrase on each index card or Post-It Note. Make enough to cover a table or whiteboard. Lay the tables out rather randomly, and then move them around until patterns emerge. When you spot a term that relates to another term put them next to each other or on top of each other. Make stacks or groups until all of the easy relationships have been found.

You'll probably have some left over, a sort of miscellaneous group, but that's okay. Look at all of the major points you were able to identify with this technique. This technique works best with concrete nouns but it is surprisingly helpful for abstract concepts too.

## Icons

Think of the signs you see at airports which use only a few signs to indicate where to go and what to do. Try making your own icons for the information you are trying to remember. Use smiley faces and simple lines. Think graphic, not art.

Here are the terms not used in the storytelling step. I'll make a graphic for some. You do the rest.

**associated pairs**
Two pears next to each other.

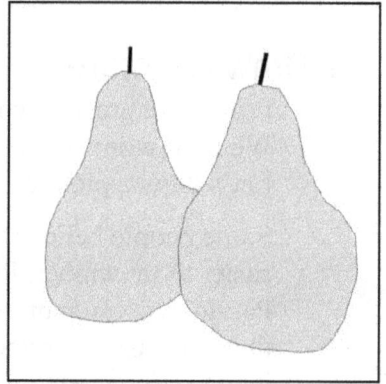

**color, size, shape, bold, underlying.**
Different font shades & sizes.

**contextual distinctiveness.**
One of these things is not like the others.

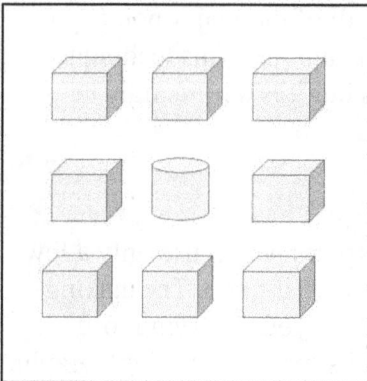

**distinctiveness**

Three types: context, $1^{st}$ time & emotional

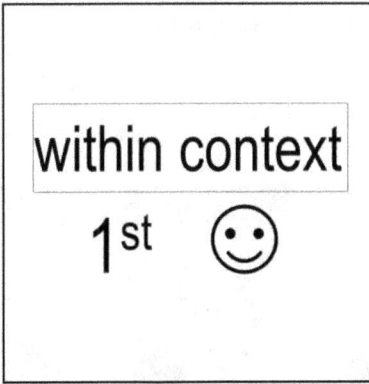

**elaboration mnemonics**

Add more to make it easier to remember

## Pictures

If you're more of an artists, your drawings could be sketches, illustrations, cartoons or paintings. If photography is your thing, find images that remind you of the terms you're trying to learn.

## Structural Overview

 These are previews of material. They tend to be graphics only. Think of them as illustrations in book or album art. They give you an idea of what is coming.

Here is a structural overview about learning being composed of facts, concepts and behaviors.

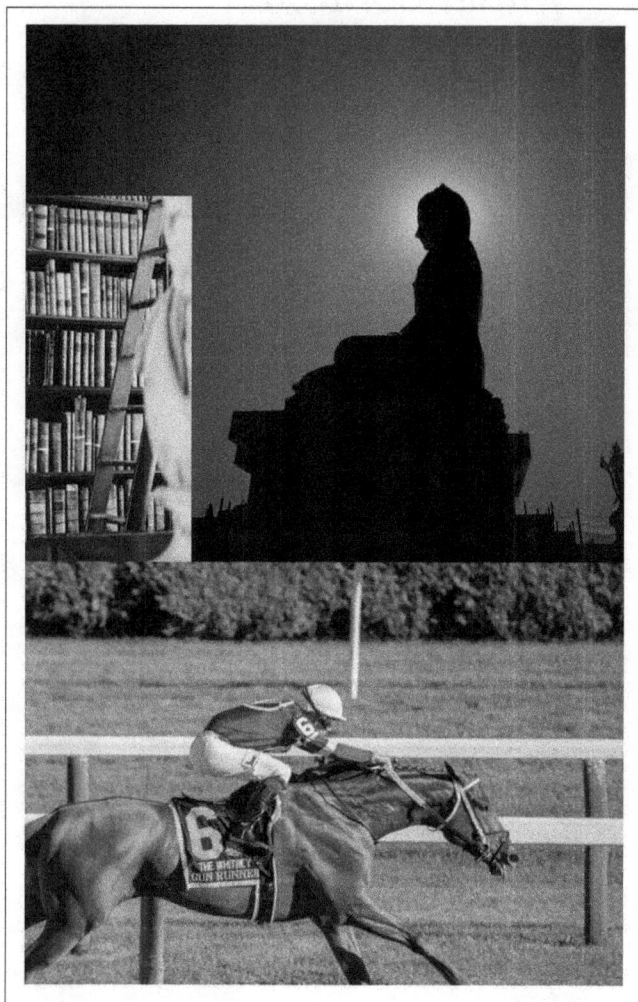

## Infographics

These are a good way to summarize a theory or explain a series of processes. They use words and pictures. Here is one I did on learning.

# LEARNING

Some learning principles apply to all animals. We all like rewards. None of use should be punished.

## HOW TO LEARN ANYTHING

### Structure Facts

We use location cues, context, distinctiveness, associations, meaningfulness and our personal assumptions to make it easier to remember facts. Individual items are hard to recall but patterns are easy for us to understand and remember.

### Illustrate Concepts

Ideas are best learned by giving multiple illustrations on one concept. We use our previous knowledge (schemas) to help categorize conceptual principles and store them as rules. We carry rules in our head so we can apply them to a wide variety of situations.

### Practice Behaviors

Practice improves our skills, shapes our behavior, and helps us replace a bad habit with a good one. Practice with rewards and feedback spread over time produces long-lasting patterns of behavior.

FACTS:

A hummingbird's wings can beat up to 200 times per second.
A crocodile can hold its breath underwater for 2 hours.
People used to cure a toothache by kissing a donkey.
Sea otters form "rafts" by holding hands.

## Mind Maps

This word-displays provide a different way of representing outlines. Some are called concept maps or words clusters but all of them give a graphic description of information Here is one I made with some of the terms about facts.

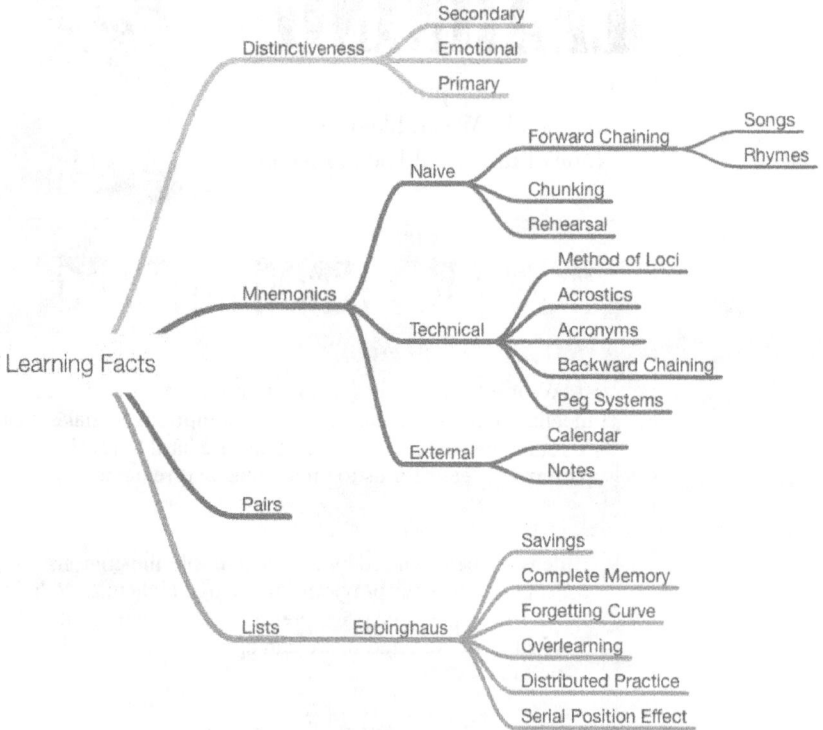

Use mind maps, infographics, clusters, drawing or anything else that makes the terms and their definitions more visual.

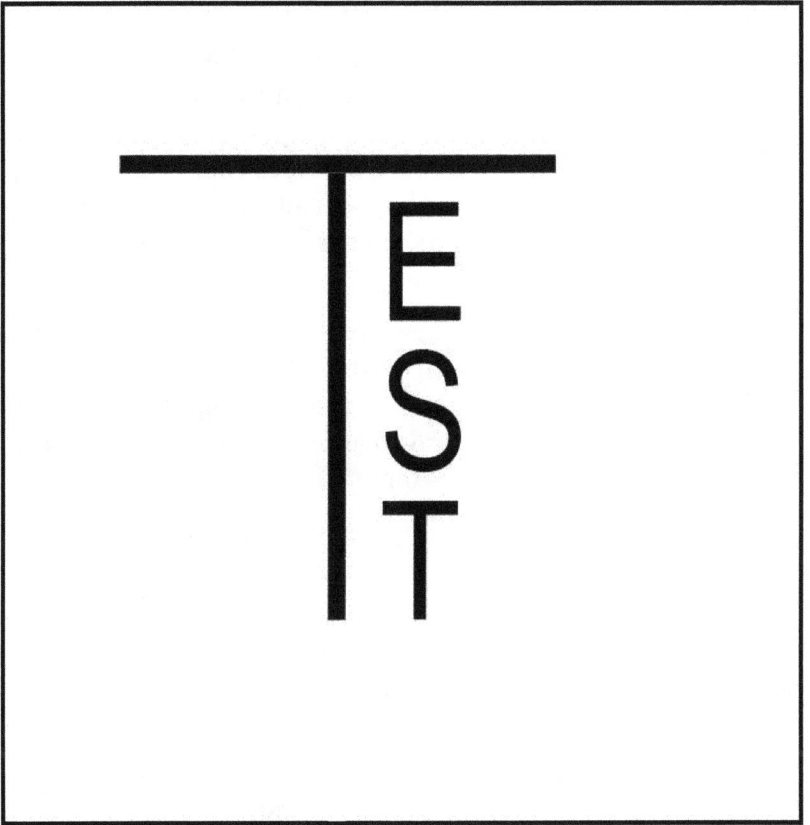

# TEST

After organizing and processing information, it is time to see if you have learned it. You won't know when you stop studying if you don't measure your performance. As a general rule, confidence precedes competence. You think you can do it before you actually can. When it comes to studying, this results in your stopping too soon. You prove your competence.

There is nothing like a dress rehearsal to show where the weak points are. This is true of plays and musicals. It is true of baseball and soccer. It is true of taking a test. The best predictor of test performance is getting a practice test that is quite similar to real thing.

Here are some ways to test your knowledge.

# 1. Flashcards

I don't know who invented flashcards but I suspect they have been around for as long as we've had paper. The advantage to flashcards is the you have to break down the material you are trying to learn into small bits, small enough to fit of a card.

Vocabular terms are a perfect fit for flashcards. The term is the cue and the definition is the response. You can quickly move through a lot of material because you are only "flashing" the cue quickly.

This is nearly the identical technique Ebbinghaus used to study memory. He wrote down a word per card, showed it to himself for 1 second, and moved on to the next card. He repeated the list over and over again.

What Ebbinghaus discovered is that lists of words that are on different topics (i.e., lists with no rational connections between items) seem like nonsense to us and are quickly forgotten. We forget random facts quickly, within a few hours. There is a rapid drop off in performance.

Ebbinghaus found three things help overcome this rapid forgetting tendency. First, he studied the list in the same order. This allows to anticipate the next cue. Think of it as a chain of associations. Practice your lists in the same order every time (at least initially). After you have mastered the material, you can shuffle the cards and consolidate your responses. But at the beginning, start by keeping the list in a single order.

Second, distribute your practice over a number of days. Don't do too much at once. It is easy to get overwhelmed and get the associations mixed up. No more than an hour a day to start with.

Third, overlearn. Don't stop when you can say the list correctly (what Ebbinghaus called "complete memory"). Keep going. The more time you spend on the cards, the better you will learn them and the better you will be able to remember them.

Use actual cards, not software. Until you're an expert flashcard user, stick with real paper. Writing the cards out will help you slow down and maintain your focus on the cards. Paper cards are also easier to shuffle into new patterns.

Once your performance is perfect, shuffle the deck and try again. Flashcards require a practice-shuffle-practice approach.

The bonds between cue and response are unidirectional. If you only flash cues and give responses, you won't be ready for test items which give you a definition and ask to you supply the cue. So, an advanced step in flashcard use is to flip the cards over and use the definitions as cues.

## 2. Teach Someone

Here is an idea that seems silly but actually works. Test your knowledge by saying it out loud. Don't do all of your studying silently. Use your voice. You can do your flashcards dramatically like a Shakespearean actor or yell them to your neighbors across the street. Or maybe just talk in a normal voice. But saying it out loud make things easier to remember.

Let's extend that idea in a technique that will help you and your classmates. Teach someone. Explaining what you know to someone else helps them but it also highlights weaknesses in your knowledge base. If you can't explain it to someone else, you don't really know it.

Don't have anyone to teach? Use your phone. You can call your mother or you can make a video of yourself giving the explanation. Either will work.

## 3. Create Your Own Tests

Before you take a test in class, create your own to test your knowledge. You don't have to be an expert at test creation. Simple tests work quite well. I think you'll be surprised that your tests aren't that much different from those your professor generates.

Here are few examples.

### Listing

List the three types of distinctiveness:

List five mnemonic techniques:

List the four types of "effects:"

**Multiple Choice**

1. The method of loci and backward chaining are both:
    a. reduction mnemonics
    b. technical mnemonics
    c. external mnemonics
    d. naïve mnemonics

2. Stimulus-response bonds are:
    a. unidirectional
    b. bidirectional
    c. lateralized
    d. centered

3. The first part of a list is remember by:
    a. reinforcement
    b. anticipation
    c. primacy
    d. recency

4. Which is a primary context distinctiveness:
    a. first time you visit New York
    b. reading a chapter a night
    c. von Restorff Effect
    d. Galen gamble

5. Who described savings and complete memory:
    a. von Restorff
    b. Ebbinghaus
    c. Aristotle
    d. Skinner

**Essay**

1. What's the difference between a naïve and a technical mnemonic?

2. Compare and contrast forward and backward chaining:

3. What are the advantages of interactive images?

# Answers

Listing

1. primary, secondary, emotional

2. method of loci, chunking, rhymes, acrostics and peg systems

3. serial position effect, von Restorff effect and the Zeigarnik effect

Multiple Choice

b, a, c, c, b

Essay

1. Naïve mnemonics are done without formal training. They include chunking, rhymes, songs, and rehearsal (saying it over and over on the way to the phone). Technical mnemonics are taught. They include method of loci, backward chaining and peg systems.

2. Forward chaining is how we usually learn a song. We start at the beginning and add things until we reach the end. We learn the first part of the list well. Backward chaining is learning the finale, then the part before and the finale, etc. We learn the last part of the list well.

3. Interactive images are the easiest to remember. The interaction forms a single combined image, lowering the demand on memory. In addition, interactive images tend to be vivid and bizarre, making them more fun.

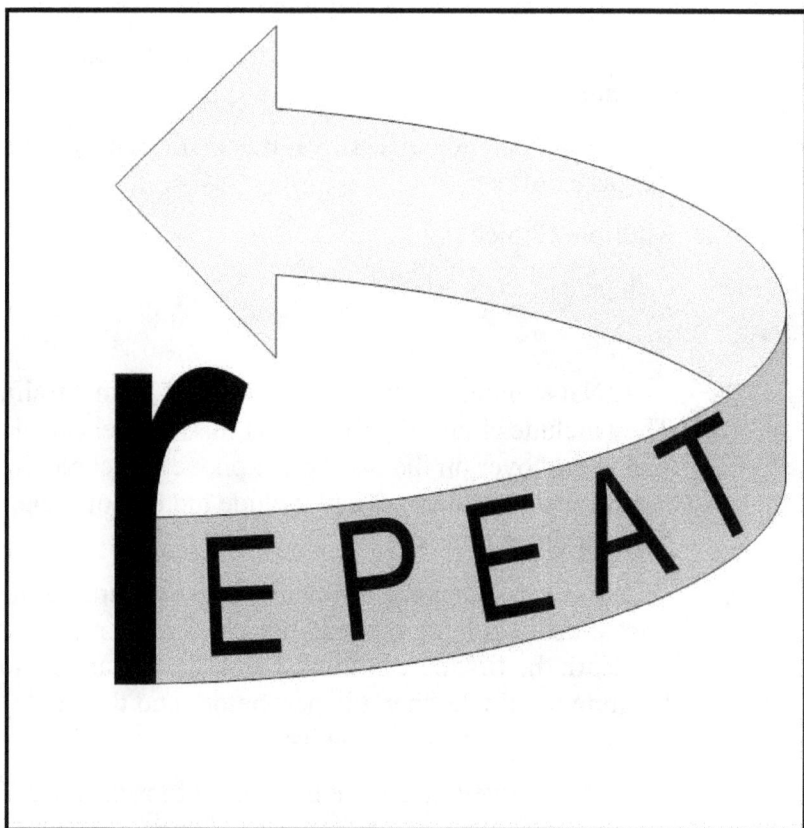

# REPEAT

## 1. Distributed Practice

Ebbinghaus confirmed what was previously generally known. He proved that the existence and form of the serial position effect. He proved that repetition is the best way to learn lists. He proved that shorter lists are easier than longer lists.

In addition to these confirmations. Ebbinghaus discover some important points. He discovered the forgetting curve, overlearning, and distributed practice. Distributed or spaced practice is the opposite of cramming. It is spacing out practice or study sessions over time. It distributes the work load.

By distributing practice, we gain in long-term retention and is speed of learning. We learn faster (fewer hours) with distributed practice and we learn better (slower forgetting).

Subsequent research shows that an hour a day provides the biggest bang for the buck. If you are trying to learn a skill, start practicing an hour a day, every day. The same seems to hold true for studying. An hour of studying a day provides enough time to understand concepts and apply them to practice problems. It is enough time to focus on memorizing facts and creating mental structures.

Studying does not include reading the textbook or taking notes in class. It does not include writing papers or completing assignments. Those tasks require additional dedicated time.

Studying is time spent organizing, processing and testing. Studying is OPT-Repeat time.

## 2. Overlearn

I previously mentioned Ebbinghaus' discovery that we do best when we go beyond confidence or complete memory. In general, we need more time than we estimate.

We often underestimate how long tasks will take. You know from your own experience that bosses often suffer from this problem. They expect a task to be done "today," even though you know that it will take three days.

It is not surprising that other people underestimate common tasks. It is more surprising that we do the same thing to ourselves. It's bad enough that other people are mean to us. It's crazy that we are mean to ourselves. We put unnecessary stress on ourselves. We push ourselves to get everything done, knowing full well that it can't be done.

Underestimating time can be part of striving for perfection. We know that it is impossible to be perfect but that doesn't stop ourselves from self-recrimination when we are less than perfect.

We often confuse familiarity for speed. We rate familiar tasks as easier than they are. This is true of gardening, accounting, cleaning and getting organized. We know what is involved but tell ourselves that it will only take a "few minutes" to clean the kitchen, pull the weeds, sort through our clothes and balance the checkbook. Or we go the other way and overestimate these tasks as "impossible" to complete.

We do the same thing with studying. We postpone writing a paper because it is overwhelming or something we can easily do riding the subway.

We study vocabulary, and feel good because we put "enough time" it. The terms look familiar. We're sure we'll be able to pick them out because the test is multiple choice. We are confident we will do well.

The familiarity of terms causes us to overestimate our competence. The test format causes us to underestimate the test's difficulty. Remember, multiple choice doesn't mean easy. Being generally aware of the material doesn't equal readiness.

Athletes do lots of drills so players don't have to think about what to do next. Try to drill your memorized knowledge (multiplication tables, periodic table of elements, historic dates, etc.). Practice it until everything flows.

Baseball players and bowlers use heavier bats and balls during practice. When they get to ready games, the equipment seems lighter and easier to use. Study for multiple choice tests as if they were listing or short answer exams. Practice as a higher level.

Keep studying. Don't stop too soon.

# 3. Avoid Flow

Flow is the felling that everything is effortless. When you're in the flow, you are "in the zone" and fully immersed. It is a mental state of being. It is great for physical activities and for meditation. Rowers and runners hit their strides. They can feel when they are in the flow. Meditation, yoga and martial arts all rely on being in the flow.

Flow is not only a mental state. It is an emotional cue. Flow is a good indicator of cognitive load. Think of it as a measure of how hard the brain is working.

In meditation and athletics, you don't want the brain to be working. You want to get out of the way. You don't want to think about this being a big day, that everything depends on you, or that they moment will change your whole life. When you're doing a sport, you want lots of flow. You want your brain disengaged.

When you're learning, you want your brain engaged. It requires brain power to hold things in working memory, pull things out of long-term memory, and make sense of a new area of knowledge. Thinking is work. You want flow to be low.

The amount of flow indicates what your brain is doing. When thinking, you want to avoid flow.

You work with flashcards until you reach flow, and beyond. For memorizing, flow is your friend. It is your goal. Keep memorizing until it is effortless.

You avoid flow when you are struggling with a new concept. If you're trying to "wrap your head around" an idea, you should not feel flow. If you feel flow when doing non-memorizing tasks, it is an indication that you should switch to a new topic. Stop studying Spanish and switch to history.

The difference between memorizing and thinking is like the difference between running and lifting weights. Running should be continuous, smooth and rhythmic. You should be in the flow. In contrast, flow should not be part of lifting weights. If you are not struggling to lift weights, they are too light. If three sets of 10 reps is easy, you increase the weight.

When you are lifting mental weights, you don't want flow. The mental floating of flow indicates you should switch to a new topic. It signals you should interleaf your topics.

Interleaving is the topical version of distributed practice. Our three sets of lifting weights is distributed practice. You work, rest, work, rest, work and stop. It is the same task distributed over time. Interleaving is distributing the topics. Our long-term performance is best when we switch from topic to topic.

If you took only one class a term, you would be used blocked practice. You study A, then B, and then C. There is no interaction or overlap between them.

If real life, you take several classes at once. You study A, write a paper for B, take a test on C, do an assignment for B, take a test for A, etc. You are using the most advanced version of interleaving: random interleaved practice. A less complicated version of interleaving is to always study ABC, ABC, and ABC. There is overlap but the topics are always in the same order. This is less effective than random interleaved practice but better than blocked practice.

Flow can help your interleaved practice. When topic A practice items are getting to easy, switch to those for topic B or C. The trick is to use flow as your trigger. When learning new material, flow signals it is time to switch.

Energy is another cue for interleaved switching. The brain gets tired from studying a single topic. With each thing we learn, there is a little build of proactive interference. Sticking new ideas in requires that old information be pushed around. It is this old information that makes it difficult to get the new stuff in. You will notice that as your study session continues, ideas become less clear and it seems harder to put things in memory. It is harder. The proactive interference is building up.

When the ideas seem to run together, switch to a new topic. You don't have to stop studying completely. Just switch to a new topic. The switch provide contrast. It makes it easier for your brain to differentiate between topic A and topic B. Interleaving also gives you more practice pulling things out of long-term memory. When you switch, you clear out working memory and load in the new topic. Think of it like restarting your computer. It clears out all of your mental caches.

When things get easy, switch.

# NEXT

You've learned how to apply the OPT-Repeat model to learning facts. We learned how to identify Don't-Knows, and practiced every step. We organized the data, processed it and tested our progress. And we did it recursively. We went through the material until we could prove we learned it. We went beyond confidence.

The next step is to do it all over again but with more terms. You've mastered facts. Now you're ready to master the rest of the psychology of learning.

# Part II

# PART 2: 1001 TERMS

In Part 1, well learned 101 terms about facts. Now, in Part 2, we are going to add 900 more, and master the entire list. We will take 1001 vocabulary terms and use the same steps: OPT-Repeat. We will organize, process, test and repeat.

I explained the steps in detail in Part 1, so in Part 2 I'll only give you light reminders of what to do.

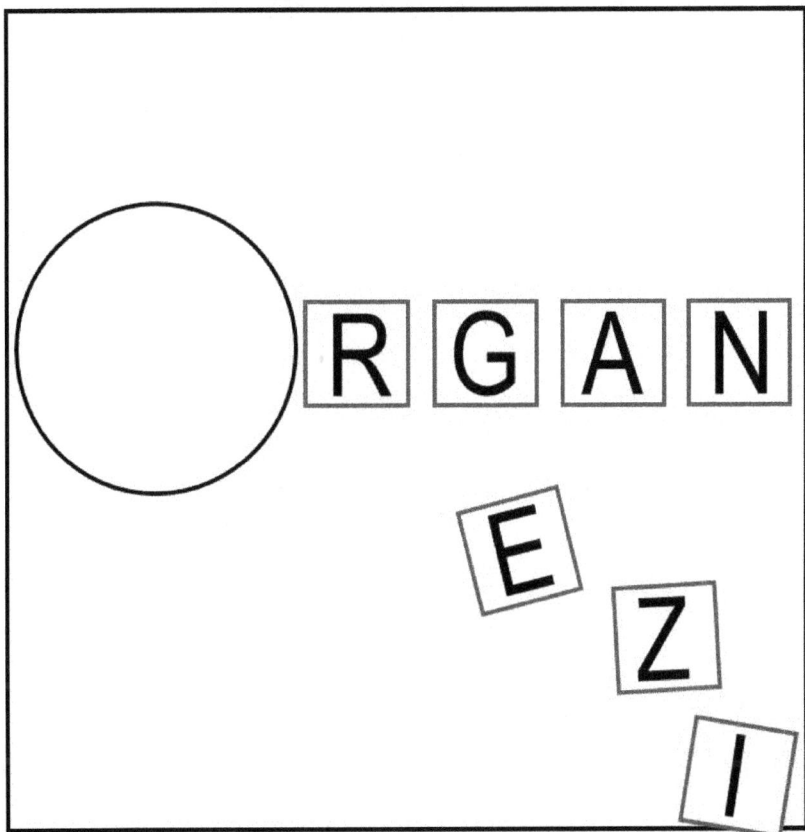

# ORGANIZE

## 1. Make A List of Don't-Knows

Positive recognition is knowing you are familiar with an item. It asks, "does anyone is this photo array look familiar." Negative recognition asks, "which faces you absolutely know you don't know." We'll use negative recognition to identify Don't-Knows. It is quick and surprisingly accurate.

The list is in a single column for easier scanning. There is enough space so you can add remarks and notations as you study.

It's a long list but it goes quickly. Don't dwell on any item. Keep it moving. You're looking for items which give you an immediate "don't know" reaction.

When in doubt, mark it and move on.

Ready?

Scan!

**1 hour a day**
**10000 hours**
**3 months**
**30 days hath September, April, June**
**5 paths to truth**
**8 Ds**
**AAA BBB CCC**
**abandonment schema**
**ABC ABC ABC**
**ABC theory of personality**
**ABCDE model**
**ABCDEFG song**
**ability**
**absolute musts**
**absolute pitch**
**abstract intelligence**
**abstract thinking**
**abstraction**
**accessible memory**
**accommodation**
**acetylcholine**
**acetylcholinesterase**
**acoustic encoding**
**acronym**
**acrostic**
**act**
**action**
**actions**
**activating event**
**active learning**
**active memory**
**active participation**
**active store**
**ad hoc methods**
**adaptation**
**adaptive behavior**
**ADHD**
**adjacent associations**
**age-dependent loss of function**

aggression
alcohol dependence
alcoholism
algorithm
all-or-none
alphabet-concrete image pegs
alphabet-rhyme pegs
alternative construction
alternatives to punishment
Alzheimer's disease
ambiguous stimuli
amnesia
amphetamine
amygdala
analogical reasoning
analogies
analytical intelligence
anchor
anecdotal evidence
animal research
animistic thinking
antecedent
antecedent condition
anterograde amnesia
anticipation
anticipatory anxiety
anxiety
applied behavior analysis
applied research
approach
approach gradient
approach-approach conflict
approach-avoidance conflict
Ariely, Dan
Aristotle
Aristotle's laws of association
assimilation
associated pairs
associated reflex

association
associationism
assumptions
atheoretical
attention
attention span
attentional bias
attitudes
attribute substitution
attribution of causality
auditory encoding
autism
autobiographical memory
automatic processing
automatization
auto-reinforcement
auto-shaping
auto-stimulation
availability heuristic
availability of strategies
available memory
aversive conditioning
avoid
avoid flow
avoidance
avoidance gradient
avoidance-avoidance conflict
awfulization
Baby Tender crib
backward chaining
backward conditioning
Baddeley, Alan
balancing skill
Bandura, Albert
bandwagon effect
Barnum effect
Bartlett, Frederic
basal ganglia
basic research

bearing cognitive map
Beck, Aaron
behavior
behavior analysis
behavior chain
behavior modification
behavior potential
behavior repertoire
behavior replication
behavior variability
behavioral change
behavioral potential
behavioral therapy
behaviorism
behaviors
Bekhterev, Vladimire
belief
belief bias
bias
big G
binding problem
black box
blank slate
blocked goals
blocked practice
blocking
Bobo the Clown
body language
bond size
bonds
bottom-up processing
bounded rationality
$BP = f(E \ \& \ RV)$
brain as a fist
brain damage
brain plasticity
brainstorming
Bransford & Johnson
breadth-first search

breaking habits
Brewer & Treyens
bridging stimulus
Bruner, Jerome
buffers
Cabrera, Derek
Calkins, Mary
calming signals
categorical variables
categories
categorization
causal attribution
causal modeling
causality
cause-effect
central executive
centration
cerebellum
cerebrum
chaining of thoughts
chains of movements
chance
characteristics of a theory
Chase & Simon
child-directed speech
childhood amnesia
childhood memories
choice
chunking
circular logic
classical conditioning
classification
clear
Clever Hans
clicker
clicker training
closed environment
clustering
Cocktail Party effect

coding
cognition
cognitive
cognitive artifacts
cognitive behaviorism
cognitive bias
cognitive development
cognitive distortions
cognitive domain
cognitive load
cognitive maps
cognitive miser
cognitive neuroscience approach
cognitive process
cognitive rule
cognitive schema
cognitive self-regulation
cognitive structures
cognitive theory
cognitive triad
cognitive-affective complexity
cognitive-developmental theory
collections of movements
color, size, shape, bold, underlying
competence
complete memory
complex environment
complex skills
conative
concept map
concepts
concrete operational stage
concrete operations
conditioned response
conditioned stimulus
conditioning
conditioning inhibition
confabulation
confidence

**confidence precedes competence**
**confirmation bias**
**conflict**
**consequence**
**conservation**
**consolidation**
**constructive alternativism**
**constructivist classroom**
**constructs**
**context**
**context analysis**
**context-dependent cues**
**context-dependent memory**
**contextual distinctiveness**
**contiguity**
**contiguous associations**
**contingency**
**continuity**
**continuous**
**continuous movement**
**continuous schedule of reinforcement**
**control processes**
**controls**
**convergent thinking**
**coping strategies**
**core irrational beliefs**
**Cornell note-taking system**
**correction**
**correlation**
**correlation coefficient**
**correspondence bias**
**cost-benefit analysis**
**counterconditioning**
**covert behavior**
**covert-unlearned**
**CPR**
**cramming**
**creative intelligence**
**creativity**

criteria
critical period
critical thinking
cross-maze
cryptomnesia
crystallized intelligence
cue
cued recall
cue-dependent forgetting
cultural schema
current moment bias
CUSS IT
CVCs
Darwin, Charles
data structures
decay theory of forgetting
decision complexity
decision fatigue
decision making
declarative memory
decoding
deductive reasoning
default setting
deferential analysis
deferred imitation
delayed matching-to-sample task
delayed retrieval
delayed-response task
deliberate practice
deliberative reasoning
delusions
demonstrable
depletion
depth-first search
derived attention
desensitization
determinants of unconscious behavior
developmental stages
differential reinforcement

**differential reinforcement of other behavior**
**differentiation**
**digestive reflexes**
**dimension**
**discovery learning**
**discrete movement**
**discrimination**
**discriminative stimulus**
**disorganized thinking**
**dissociate fugue**
**dissociative amnesia**
**distance**
**distinctions**
**distinctiveness**
**distorted memory**
**distorting effects**
**distractions**
**distributed practice**
**divergent thinking**
**divide and conquer**
**doctrine of formal discipline**
**Dollard & Miller**
**Dollard & Miller therapy**
**don't forget**
**don't punish**
**doodling**
**dopamine**
**double approach-avoidance conflict**
**double-blind study**
**draw a picture of the problem situation**
**dress rehearsal**
**drive**
**drive reduction**
**drive, cue, response, reward**
**driving range**
**drugs**
**dry tech rehearsal**
**duration**
**dynamic stereotype**

early selection
Ebbinghaus, Hermann
echoic memory
economy of motion
effect
egg and spear technique
egocentric
eidetic memory
elaboration mnemonics
elicited
Ellis, Albert
emitted
emotional distinctiveness
emotional disturbance
emotional intelligence
emotional memories
emotional self-regulation
emotions facilitate behavior
empathy gap
empiricism
empty gap
encoding
encoding specificity principle
engagement
entorhinal cortex
environment
environmental cues
environmental reinforcer
epinephrine
episodic buffer
episodic memory
epistemic cognition
escape learning
eugenics
event marker
excessive punishment
executive process
exercise
expanded retrieval strategy

expectation
expectation schema
experimental neurosis
experts
explicit memory
external locus of control
external mnemonics
externally-paced events
external-paced events
extinction
extinction burst
eye witness testimony
face recognition
facts
fading
false memory
far transfer
fast and frugal
fatigue method
fear conditioning
feedback
fictions
fine motor skills
FITS
fixed interval
fixed ratio
fixed theory of intelligence
flashcards
flooded with memories
flooding method
flow
fluid intelligence
fluid movements
focus
focusing effect
forgetting
forgetting curve
formal operational stage
forward chaining

forward conditioning
four common problem-solving strategies
four consequences of punishment
frame
framing
framing effect
free recall
free will
frequency
frustration
frustration-aggression hypothesis
functional analysis
functional explanation
functional fixedness
fundamental attribution error
fuzzy-headed thinking
Galton, Francis
gambler's fallacy
game theory
Gardner, Howard
gender schema theory
general intelligence
Gigerenzer, Gerd
goal setting
goal state
goals
Google effect
gradient of approach
gradient of avoidance
Grandma's law
gross motor skills
GROW
Guthrie, Edwin
habit
habit formation
habit loop
habit strength
half a biscuit for the same job
half-second

halo effect
HAM
heuristics
hierarchy of needs
hierarchy of response
higher criteria
high-level form of learning
highlighted foreground
hill climbing
hindsight bias
hot cognition
how to learn lists
Hull, Clark
human reflexology
hypothesis testing
Hypothetico-Deductive Theory
iconic memory
ideas
identical elements
idiographic
IKEA effect
ill-defined problems
illumination
imageless thought
images
imitation
immediate gain
implicit memory
implosive desensitization
impressions
imprinting
inattentional blindness
incentive
incidental encoding
incompatible behavior
incompatible response method
incremental theory of intelligence
incubation
infantile amnesia

infographic
instinctive drift
instincts
instrumental conditioning
intelligence
intelligence quotient
intelligence test
intensity
intent
intentional behavior
interactional synchrony
interactive images
interference theory
interleafed practice
intermittent schedules
internal locus of control
internally consistent
inter-stimulus interval
interval schedules
intervening events
introspection
involuntary attention
irradiation
irrational beliefs
irreversibility
isomorphism
item familiarity
item similarity
jackpot
Jacobs, Joseph
James, William
Jones, Mary
journey method
Kahneman, Daniel
keep-going signal
Kelly, George
knowledge
labels
Lake Wobegone effect

language acquisition device
language development
late selection
latency
latent inhibition
latent learning
lateral thinking
law of effect
law of exercise
law of readiness
laws
laws of association
learned helplessness
learned optimism
learning
learning by doing
learning process
level of initial learning
lexical retrieval
link & story systems
list length
Little Albert
little g
live fire
LMNOP
lobes
local high
location cues
Locke, John
locus of control
Loftus, Elizabeth
longitudinal research design
long-term memory
loop theory of habits
loss aversion
low-level form of learning
magical thinking
masking
Maslow, Abraham

Maslow's hammer
massed practice
maximum certainly
maximum fluency
meaning extraction
meaningful
means-end analysis
mechanical intelligence
memory
memory characteristics
memory palace
memory systems
mental inactivity
mental rehearsal
mental representation
mental retardation
mental set
mental strategies
mental structures
mental tests
metacognition
metaphors
method of focal objects
method of loci
methylphenidate
Miller, George
mind as a computer analogy
mind map
mindfulness
minimum energy
minimum time
mirroring
misery-stupidity syndrome
misinformation effect
mixed movements
mixed practice
mixed skills
mnemonics
modeling

modeling therapy
models
morphological analysis
motivation
motives
movement
movement produced stimuli
multiple contexts
multiple memory systems
muscle memory
naieve mnemonics
name recognition
naturalistic observation
near transfer
negate
negative punishment
negative recognition
negative reinforcement
neglect of probability
neural plasticity
neurosis
nicknames
no reward marker
Noh theater
nonsense words
non-synaptic plasticity
normal practice
normalcy bias
note taking
number of decision options
number-rhyme reversal system
number-rhyme system
object classification
object permanence
object schemas
observational learning
one-shot learning
open environment
operant

operant conditioning
operant conditioning chamber
operational definition
opposites
order of presentation
ordinal relationships
outline
overestimate transfer of learning
overlearning
overt behaviors
pace
panic attack
panic disorder
partial reinforcement
part-set cuing
passive store
past punishment
path integration
Pavlov, Ivan
PDCA
peg systems
performance characteristics
permastores
perseverance
perseveration
person as scientist
person schemas
personal construct theory
personal constructs
personal experience
personality
pessimistic style of thinking
phonological loop
photographic memory
photographs
physical monism
Piaget, Jean
picture superiority effect
pie chart models

pillory
placebo effect
plan for failure
plasticity
pleasure
Pollyanna effect
positive punishment
positive recognition
positive reinforcement
post-purchase rationalization
practical intelligence
practical memory
practical problem solving
practice
practice effects
practice sessions
praise and affection
predictably irrational
Premack principle
preoperational intelligence
preoperational stage of development
preoperational thinking
preparation
prerequisites for good decision making
primacy
primary distinctiveness
primary drives
primary memory
primary reinforcer
priming
proactive interference
problem definition
problem finding
problem shaping
problem space
problem state
problem-solving opportunity
procedural memory
productive failure

programmed instruction
programmed learning
proportional reward
propositional thought
proprioceptive stimuli
prospective memory
proverbs
proximal zone of development
proximity
psychic secretions
punishment
punishment marker
purposeful behaviorism
puzzle box
pyramid models
qualitative research
quantitative research
RADAR
rapid verbal, slow motor forgetting
ratio schedule
rational choice theory
rational emotive behavioral therapy
rational emotive therapy
rational psychotherapy
rationality
RDO
reasoning
recall
recency
reciprocal altruism
recognition
recognition errors
recollection
reconsolidation
reduction
reduction mnemonics
reframing
rehearsal
reinforcement

reinforcement
reinforcement
reinforcement value
reinstatement
reinstatement of context
release from proactive interference
reminiscence
repetition
representation of knowledge
repressed memory
research
resilience
resistance to forgetting
response
rest
retention
retrieval failure
retrieve often
retroactive interference
retrograde analysis
review
reward
reward marker
reward size
rewrite your notes
rhinal cortices
rhymes
robust effect
root-cause analysis
rooting
rote learning
Rotter, Julian
Rotter's formula
rule of thumb
Rumpelstiltskin effect
saccade
same order every time
satisficing
savings

scaffolding
scalloped
schedules of reinforcement
schema
schema characteristics
schema development
schema hierarchy
schema limits
schema uses
scripts
secondary attention
secondary circular reactions
secondary distinctiveness
secondary drives
secondary reinforcer
self-control therapy
self-discipline
self-efficacy
self-paced events
self-punishment
self-regulation
self-reinforcement
self-schemas
self-stimulation of the brain
self-sustaining schema
self-talk
semantic encoding
semantic memory
sensorimotor stage
sensory memory
sentence completion
sequential models
serial interleaving
serial movements
serial position effect
serial recall
sham-feeding
shaping
sheltered workshops

short-term memory
shuttle box
side effects
sidetracking method
sign tracking
similar dimensions
similarity
Simon, Herbert
Simonides of Ceos
simple skills
single subject designs
single-blind study
six steps of problem solving
sketch cognitive map
Skinner, BF
small number of assumptions
social intelligence
social learning theory
social psychology
sounds like
source amnesia
source monitoring
sparse encoding
spatial memory
spatial reasoning
speeded tests
split-brain people
spontaneous recovery
spotlight effect
spread of effect
S-R
stamped in
stamped out
state variables
state-dependent learning
status-quo bias
stereotypes
stimulus generalization
store recipes

storyboard
straight-run maze
stress
string on your finger
Stroop effect
structural overview
study skills
stupidity-misery syndrome
subvocalized speech
successive approximations
summarizes facts
superstitious behavior
suppressed background
switch tasks
systematic desensitization
tactile encoding
talent
Tangen's two principles of human behavior
target behaviors
target contexts
target skills
target stick
task analysis
taste aversion
teach someone
teaching machine
technical mnemonics
test self
testable hypotheses
thinning
Thorndike, Edward
thoughts
three things you can learn
threshold method
time out
time-gap
tip of tongue phenomenon
token economy
Tolman, Edward

**top-down processing**
**total time hypothesis**
**Tower of Hanoi**
**trace conditioning**
**trace decay theory**
**track, try & reward strategy**
**tracking**
**trained mind**
**transfer of training**
**translation schemes**
**trial and error learning**
**triarchic theory of successful intelligence**
**triggers**
**triple-blind study**
**Tulving, Endel**
**two as a swan**
**two-factor theory of intelligence**
**two-fer**
**unconditioned response**
**unconditioned stimulus**
**unidirectional bonds**
**unlabeled conflicts**
**unresolved conflicts**
**useful**
**variable interval**
**variable ratio**
**variables**
**vector-based cognitive map**
**verbal intelligence**
**verbal reports**
**verification**
**vicarious learning**
**vicarious punishment**
**vicarious reinforcement**
**visual encoding**
**visualization**
**visuo-spatial sketchpad**
**vividness**
**voluntary behavior**

von Restorff Effect
Vygotsky, Lev
waiting room experiment
War of the Ghosts
warm up trials
Watson, John
wax tablet
well-defined problems
white rat psychologist
Williams, Ted
withdrawal
within list associations
word association
word lists
word pairs
word-completion items
work
workflow
working memory
working problems backwards
worldview
write it down
writer's cramp
Wundt, Wilhelm
Ye & Salvendy
Zeigarnik Effect

## 2. Make A List of Things Likely to Be on The Test

Use the Rule of Three (class, notes and book) as your starting point. Identify words and phrases you think are Likely-On-Test items.

Another tip is to look for names which repeat. If there are a lot of terms related to Dollard & Miller, Skinner and Ebbinghaus, those names and terms are likely to be on the test.

# 3. Make A List by Categories

Use categories to help you organize the material. Time lines, dates, similarities, people you agree with, theories you hate…. Use any category you can think of.

Here is a list of theorists who are mentioned directly or indirectly in the glossary.

**Ariely, Dan**
**Aristotle**
**Baddeley, Alan**
**Bahrick, Harry**
**Bandura, Albert**
**Barnum, PT** (Barnum effect)
**Bartlett, Frederic**
**Beck, Aaron**
**Bekhterev, Vladimire** (associated reflex)
**Bobo the Clown**
**Bransford & Johnson** (serenading a woman)
**Brewer & Treyens** (waiting room)
**Broadbent, Donald** (cocktail party effect)
**Bruner, Jerome**
**Cabrera, Derek**
**Calkins, Mary**
**Cattell, James McKeen**
**Cattell, Raymond**
**Chase & Simon**
**Clever Hans** (the horse)
**Cornell** (university note taking system)
**Craik & Lockhart** (depth of processing theory)
**Darwin, Charles**
**Descartes**
**Dewey, John**
**Dollard & Miller**
**Ebbinghaus, Hermann**
**Ellis, Albert**
**Forer, Bertrum** (Forer effect)

**Freud, Sigmund**
**Galileo**
**Galton, Francis**
**Gardner, Howard**
**Gigerenzer, Gerd** (fast and frugal decision making)
**Gilbert, Daniel** (empathy gap)
**Gladwell, Malcolm** (10,000 hours)
**Grandma** (contingency)
**Guthrie, Edwin**
**Hobbes, Thomas**
**Holmes, Sherlock**
**Hull, Clark**
**Jacobs, Joseph**
**James, William** (21 days to make a habit)
**Jones, Mary** (behavior therapy)
**Kahneman, Daniel**
**Keillor, Garrison**
**Kelly, George**
**Korsakoff's syndrome**
**Lewin, Kurt**
**Little Albert**
**Locke, John** (blank slate, trained mind)
**Loftus, Elizabeth** (eye-witness testimony)
**Marbe, Karl** (mental set)
**Maslow, Abraham**
**Miller, George**
**Murray, Henry** (TAT personality test)
**Osten, Wilheim van** (horse trainer)
**Pavlov, Ivan**
**Piaget, Jean**
**Rogers, Carl**
**Rotter, Julian**
**Rugaas, Turid** (calming signals)
**Rumpelstiltskin**
**Seligman, Martin**
**Simon, Herbert** (bounded rationality)
**Simonides of Ceos**
**Skinner, BF**
**Spearman, Charles** (general intelligence)

**Sternberg, Robert**
**Stroop, John** (Stroop effect)
**Tangen, Ken**
**Thorndike, Edward**
**Titchener, Edward** (structuralism)
**Tolman, Edward**
**Tulving, Endel**
**Tversky & Kahneman** (loss aversion)
**von Restorff, Hedwig** (von Restorff effect)
**Vygotsky, Lev**
**Watson, John**
**Williams, Ted** (baseball player)
**Wolpe, Joseph** (systematic desensitization)
**Wundt, Wilhelm**
**Ye & Salvendy**
**Zeigarnik, Bluma** (Zeigarnik effect)

## 4. Make A List of Personal Interests

In the process of learning things to do well on tests and get through classes, don't forget to jot down things you might want to explore in the future when you have more time. Make a list of things that for your personal growth or general interest. It is good to have a Someday list.

# PROCESS

# PROCESS

## 1. Look Up Don't-Knows

Now that we've identified the Don't-Knows, we convert them to Sort-Of-Knows. Look up the definitions for the terms you don't know in the **Glossary**.

## 2. Write A Story

It is unreasonable to put 1001 terms in a single story. So, there are two approaches you can take here. First, you can select a group of terms that all relate to each other. For example, you could take all of the terms related to Skinner or operant conditioning. The advantage is that they all relate to each other. This allow you to make fine distinctions between closely related terms. The disadvantage is you can compare and contrast terms from Skinner with those from Pavlov.

Second, take a random selection of terms. This will allow you make broad distinctions between theorists and approaches. The down side is that the finer within-topic distinctions will be harder to make.

Best bet: do both.

## 3. Draw A Picture

Although you can visually encode 1001 terms, you can still use visualization. As with words, your choice is to select items randomly or pick a subset of terms that all relate to each other. Both will be improved by visually representing them. It makes it easy to find relationships you didn't know existed.

Best bet: use both approaches. Make a visual of random items. Make one or more visuals for the most important subtopics in the material (Skinner, Pavlov, Ebbinghaus, etc.).

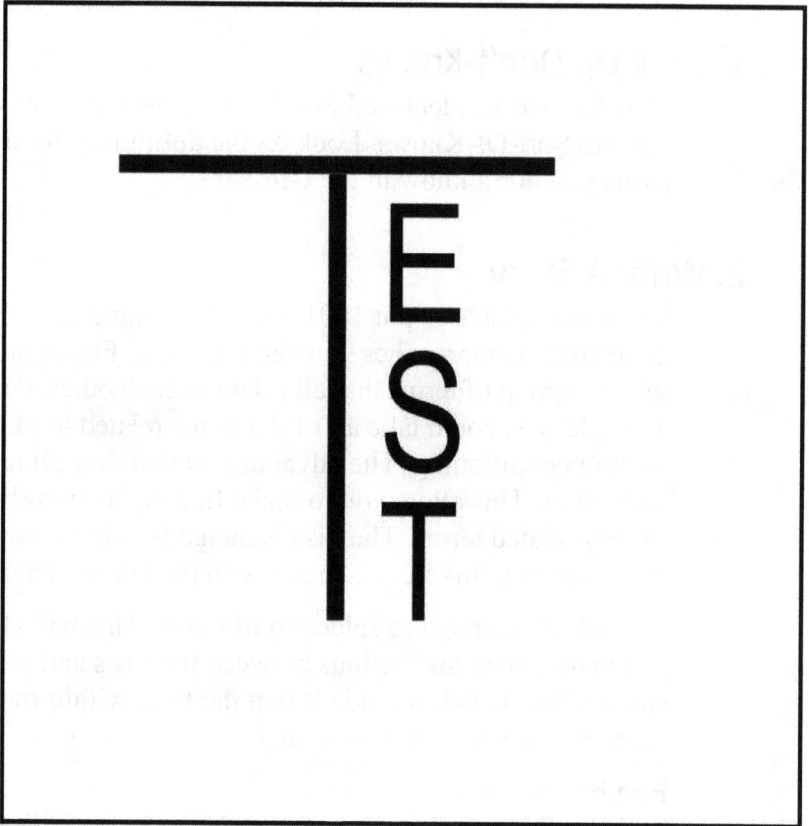

# TEST

## 1. Flashcards

Make flashcards the way the ancient Greeks did: by hand. I made that up but since they didn't have computers I'm sure that if they had flashcards they made them by hand.

Do it the old-fashioned way. Slow down your thinking. Stop rushing around. Grab a stack of index cards and a pen. One term (and definition) per card. Take the definitions I give you and make them your own by paraphrasing them. The best approach is to put things in your own words.

You can add drawings and doodles too. Include anything that will help you remember the material better. Then, practice, shuffle, practice.

## 2. Teach Someone

Teaching others is more for you than for them. Teaching others in your study group will help them but it will help you more. When you explain something out loud you have to generate the language for it. You've got to come up with what to say and how to say it. The generation process helps solidify what you know and highlights the parts you don't know well enough.

## 3. Create Your Own Tests

Write your own tests. They can be essay, listing, matching or multiple choice. The choice is up to you.

The best bet is to use the same format your prof will use. If they like essay tests, practice making essay tests (and answers). If you'll be tested with multiple choice items, making listing, sentence completion and multiple choice tests for yourself.

Here is how to take a multiple choice test. The stem of a multiple choice item (the words before the list of options) should be thought of as a sentence completion question. First, before you look at the option, try to fill in the blank. Second, find the answer that matches your initial response. Consequently, the best way to study for a multiple choice test is multiple choice items, sentence completion items and lists.

## Example Test

1. People are really good at recognizing:
     a. upside-down faces
     b. sideways faces
     c. upright faces
     d. inkblots

2. A wax tablet is one of the oldest metaphors for:
     a. associations
     b. sensation
     c. memory
     d. artistry

3. Which is a naïve mnemonic:
     a. writing things down
     b. method of loci
     c. chunking
     d. all of the above

4. According to Tangen, there are only three things you can learn:
     a. facts, concepts and behaviors
     b. facts, attitudes and schemas
     c. skills, attitudes and dates
     d. skills, habits and acts

5. According to Calkins, the largest impact on memory is:
     a. frequency of presentation
     b. vividness of images
     c. symmetry
     d. recency

6. Retracing your steps to remember something is trying to activate:
     a. state dependent cues
     b. location cues
     c. far transfer
     d. flooding

7. In video games, when you need to remember where you are and who to zap next you are using:
   a. working memory
   b. semantic memory
   c. episodic memory
   d. procedural memory

8. When you are sad to tend to remember:
   a. funny things
   b. happy things
   c. noble things
   d. sad things

9. Everything looks like a nail, according to:
   a. Maslow's hammer
   b. phi phenomenon
   c. scaffolding
   d. mental set

10. Deciding why you broke up with your spouse is an:
    a. bounded rationality
    b. ill-defined problem
    c. connectionism
    d. hindsight bias

11. For Thorndike, incorrect responses are:
    a. stamped out
    b. stamped in
    c. lateralized
    d. fracture

12. Lack of knowing what your competitor will do is an example of:
    a. bounded rationality
    b. ill-defined problem
    c. connectionism
    d. hindsight bias

1

3. Like rats, when we like something we:
   a. approach it
   b. ignore it
   c. attack it
   d. avoid it

14. When Dollard & Miller say "stupid" they mean:
   a. unrewarded
   b. reinforced
   c. conflicted
   d. unlabeled

15. Too many decisions, regardless of complexity, causes:
   a. decision fatigue
   b. trial and error
   c. satisficing
   d. anchors

16. Which reevaluates at each step toward a goal:
   a. means-end analysis
   b. randomization
   c. trial and error
   d. law of effect

17. Bahrick showed that memory for names and faces:
   a. increases over time
   b. increases with age
   c. drops off steadily
   d. drops off rapidly

18. AAA BBB CCC is the pattern of:
   a. distributed interleafing
   b. random interleafing
   c. serial interleafing
   d. blocked practice

19. There are only three things you can learn:
    a. facts
    b. concepts
    c. behaviors
    d. all of the above

20. Which only occurs after extinction:
    a. spontaneous recovery
    b. antecedent beliefs
    c. discrimination
    d. blocking

21. Sitting on a stool to think about what you've done wrong is:
    a. negative reinforcement
    b. positive reinforcement
    c. negative punishment
    d. positive punishment

22. Which is a combination of positive punishment and negative punishment:
    a. spanking in the woodshed
    b. confined to your room
    c. can't go to the dance
    d. public pillory

23. Operant conditioning only works if the reward is:
    a. contingent
    b. thoughtful
    c. intentional
    d. deliberate

24. At what point does additional practice probably not make much difference:
    a. 1 hour per day
    b. 2 hours per day
    c. 3 hours per day
    d. 4 hours per day

25. Exploring all of the branches at one level before exploring further down is:
    a. trial and error search
    b. breadth-first search
    c. leaf & stem search
    d. depth-first search

## Listing Items

1. List the four ways to break a habit:

2. List the five schedules of reinforcement:

3. List the four components of classical conditioning:

**Essay Items**

1. What happens after a reward is no longer given.

2. Compare and contrast classical and operant conditioning.

3. Compare and contrast schemas and scripts.

# Answers

## Multiple Choice:

a, c, c, a, a, b, a, d, a, b, a, a, a,
d, a, a, d, d, d, a, c, d, a, d, b

## Listing items:

1. flooding, incompatible response, threshold, sidetracking

2. continuous, fixed interval, fixed ratio, variable interval, variable ratio

3. unconditioned stimulus, unconditioned response, conditioned stimulus, conditioned response

## Essay items:

1. First there will be an extinction burst, where the behavior is increased. Second, if the behavior is not rewarded, the behavior will gradually decrease to extinction. Third, after some time, spontaneous recovery will occur, followed by re-extinction.

2. Classical conditioning is based on reflexes. When two stimuli are paired together an association bond is developed. Once the bond is established, a previously neural stimulus will elicit a response that is similar to an unconditioned response. Operant conditioning is based on consequences which follow behavior. Behaviors are constantly emitted. Some are rewarded and will become more likely to occur. Rewards impact operants (whole class of behaviors).

3. Schemas are a broad category of mental structures which included scripts. Schemas were first introduced by Jean Piaget to describe the types of thinking people have. Piaget believed that the ability to form and use schema developed in stages as children grow. The term schema

became more broadly applied as different theorists proposed alternative uses for the word. Bartlett's War of Ghosts study showed we distort new information to fit with existing schemas, which is similar to Piaget's use of accommodation and assimilation.

# REPEAT

## 1. Distributed Practice

Distributing your work load makes learning easier. Don't do it all at once. Learning is quicker and better if spaced out over time. Try to do some every day.

## 2. Overlearn

Stop studying when you can prove you know it. Don't stop when you're confident. Keep going until you are competent. Overlearn beyond "I think I can." Stop only when you can show you can.

## 3. Avoid Flow

Use flow as a cue. If you're meditating, aim to maximize flow. If you're studying, aim to minimize flow. Don't study on autopilot. Keep the brain working hard by changing to another topic.

# Glossary

# GLOSSARY

**#**

**1 hour a day**. The amount of time per day needed to become an expert, assuming one daily session every day for ten years is spent using deliberate practice.

**10000 hours**. The idea popularized by Malcolm Gladwell that to become an expert, it takes 10000 hours of deliberate practice. Shows the most promise in well structures environments (such as chess and classical music). Seems to vary greatly by domain.

**3 months**. There is no agreed-upon amount of time to acquire a habit but for most people 3 months is probably about right. William James suggested 21 days, some people take a full year. The appropriate amount varies greatly with the person and the habit being formed.

**30 days**. Part of "30 days hath September, April, June…" A rhyming mnemonic, an effective naïve mnemonic.

**5 paths to truth**. Tangen's summary of methods people use to find truth. They include religion (revelation), wisdom (insight), philosophy (logic), science (systematic observation) and chance (dumb luck).

**8 Ds**. A problem solving strategy developed by Ford Motor Company. The eight disciplines (8Ds) are designed for teams and include: use a team, describe the problem, containment plan, root causes, permanent corrections, implementation, prevent reoccurrences, and congratulate your team.

# A

**AAA BBB CCC**. The pattern used in blocked practice. Task A is learned, then B and then C.

abandonment schema    A way of looking at life, based on personal experience. Assumes everyone will leave you.

**ABC ABC ABC**. The pattern used in interleafed practice. This is a sequential interleafed pattern where A is always practiced before B, etc. Good for long-term memory. A random interleafed pattern is usually even better.

**ABC theory of personality**. According to Ellis, personality is learned. Personality is defined a dynamic interrelationship of activating events, beliefs and consequences (feelings). Since you can't change the world's activating events (A), change your beliefs (B) and feelings (C) will change. If you don't like your personality, change your beliefs.

**ABCDE model**. Seligman's version of Albert Ellis' distorted thinking model. Stands for Adversity, Beliefs, Consequences, Disputation of belief, and Energization.

**ABCDEFG song**. An example of forward chaining. We learn the first part of the song best; worse as you get to middle.

**ability**. Innate skill. Usually not a good predictor of success. Time spent practicing is a better predictor.

**absolute musts**. Ellis says we fool ourselves into believing that things must absolutely occur one way or another. Instead of saying we prefer that we don't lose a job, we say we absolutely must not lose a job. We overstate the importance of circumstances.

**absolute pitch**. Also called perfect pitch or pitch recognition. Originally thought an innate skill but most people can achieve it with practice.

**abstract intelligence**. Similar to Piaget's formal operations or Raymond Cattell's fluid intelligence. Includes the use of symbols, pattern recognition, and seeing things within context.

**abstract thinking**. In contrast to concrete thinking, abstract thinking uses formal operations of logic. Includes the manipulation of words and concepts. You can use symbols and think things through in your head. Called formal operational thinking by Piaget.

**abstraction**. The use of model (mental or physical) to test out ideas before creating real life structures. Maps are abstractions of a place's geography. Art that looks less realistic.

**accessible memory**. In contrast to available memory (what is stored), accessible memory describes what can be retrieved. Think of a stuffed, messy tool shed which holds all of your tools. You know there is hammer in there somewhere (it is available) but it is not easily accessible. It is easier to borrow one from your neighbor than search through your shed.

**accommodation**. For Piaget, adding of new schema categories. In a card catalog it would be creating a new card. In contrast to assimilation (adding more information to the categories you already have).

**acetylcholine** (ACh). Neurotransmitter needed to encode new memories. Produced primarily in the basal forebrain (nucleus basalis of Meynert). Acetylcholine deletion is an early sign of Alzheimer's disease.

**acetylcholinesterase**. Abbreviated AChE) Hormone that breaks down acetylcholine. Inhibiting this enzyme is being investigated as a treatment for the early stage of Alzheimer's.

**acoustic encoding**. Air waves are transduced into to neural impulses. The information is processed in a series of concentric circles in the temporal lobe and stored (somewhere unknown) in a sparse encode (a neural abstraction of the original sounds).

**acronym**. A reduction mnemonic which shortens a series of words into a series of letters. American Broadcasting Company becomes ABC. Regular Day Off becomes RDO. Radio Detection And Ranging becomes RADAR (RAdio Detection And Ranging). Unlike acrostics, the letter must stay in the same order.

**acrostic**. A reduction mnemonic which creates a new word out of the initial letters of a group of words. The order of the letters can be changed to optimize its effectiveness. The personality dimensions for the Big Five can be CANOE or OCEAN, whichever is preferred. Helpful for remember the number and order of items. Not helpful for remembering the desired underlying terms.

**act**. A behavior. For Guthrie, an act is a collection of movements. Brentano's "act psychology" rejected the mind as a passive recipient of sensations; emphasized the importance of mental acts. Carr described behavior as an adaptive act (adjusting to needs).

**action**. People are quite easily distracted by motion. Any action makes things more interest but we're particularly responsive to curved action. Magicians distract use by moving one hand in an arc while performing their magic with the other hand.

**actions**. Behaviors, everything you do.

**activating event**. In cognitive behavioral theory, an environmental stimulus that triggers a belief with in turn triggers an emotion.

**active learning**. Also called purposive, engaged or situation-driven learning. The emphasis is on the learner directing and being responsible for constructing their own learning. Theorists include Jerome Bruner (discovery learning), Bandura and Vygotsky.

**active memory**. Also called short-term or working memory. Limited memory for seven items (plus or minus two). Rehearsal keeps items in consciousness.

**active participation**. A component of Vygotsky's approach to learning, along with immediate feedback, peer collaboration and assisted discovery. Active participation is the requirement that children do things as they pursue learning. Learning occurs within a social context where mentors help guide children's exploration with object and tasks.

**active store**. In theory, a place where we temporarily store and process information. Working memory is often described as an active store.

**ad hoc methods**. Creating solutions for specific tasks, not more generalized mental representations.

**adaptation**. All senses except pain quickly adjust to new level; less responsive. Two doses of sour; first is perceived as more sour.

**adaptive behavior**. Behaviors that help fill the needs of both the child and their teacher, parents and others. Typically, every day skills and self-care behaviors: effective communication, handling money, and problem solving. Find ways to get around your disability.

**ADHD**. An abbreviation of attention deficit hyperactivity disorder). Developmental disorder which impacts learning. Symptoms include difficulty inhibiting behavior, focusing attention and being patient. Tend to be motivated by things that interest them but highly unmotivated for other tasks. Can be diagnosed as hyperactive-impulsive or inattentive or both.

Cause is unknown but seems to include impaired processing of dopamine and norepinephrine, overdeveloped motor cortex, underdeveloped prefrontal cortex (left side), underdeveloped posterior parietal lobe, and decreased limbic system activity (striatum to prefrontal cortex connections). Symptoms improve as the brain grows but continue to have lifelong effect. Often treated with low doses of stimulants and therapy. The drugs aim to improve attention; therapy aims to tend self-control and coping skills.

**adjacent associations**. For Ebbinghaus, items that have associations with other items on a list are easier to learn. List with items close or next to each other (adjacent) are even easier to learn.

**age-dependent loss of function**. The premise that everything in the body, including memory, gets worse as you age.

**aggression**. The readiness to inflict harm. For Dollard & Miller, frustration is caused by goals being blocked.

**alcohol dependence**. Physical and/or psychological need to drink alcohol.

**alcoholism**. Problem drinking caused by learning, genetics or a combination of factors.

**algorithm**. In contrast to a heuristic or rule. Algorithms are formulas, which might be slow but will produce the correct solution.

**all-or-none**. For Guthrie, learning occurs all or none. Small movements are learned in one shot. But there are so many small movements that learning appears to be gradual.

**alphabet-concrete image pegs**. A technical mnemonic technique that uses concrete images that start with the same letter. A is ape or apple, b is boy, c is cat or cot or car, etc.

**alphabet-rhyme pegs**. A technical mnemonic technique used to spell words. Pegs are based on sound-alikes. A is hay or ale. B is bee. C is see. Not as widely used as concrete image pegs because some rhymes are difficult to create.

**alternative construction**. Kelly suggestion that when a construct isn't working for you, select an alternative. Believe something different. Learn to become what you want to be.

**alternatives to punishment**. Instead of punishing, you can use mediation, negotiation, barter, or have a contest that rewards positive behaviors (such as creativity or empathy).

**Alzheimer's disease**. Most common type of dementia, cause unknown. Results in impaired learning and permanent memory loss.

**ambiguous stimuli**. A stimulus whose edges or characteristics are difficult to define, making discriminations difficult. Common in real life.

**amnesia**. Loss of memory, temporarily or permanently. Includes retrograde (what happened before the crash), anterograde (what happened after the crash) and source amnesia (don't know where I read that).

**amphetamine**. A synthesized stimulant that is taken to increase alertness, and for its euphoric effect. Easily abused; can get hooked on a single dose.

**amygdala**. The connection between the cortex (thinking) and the limbic system (feeling).

**analogical reasoning**. Using "this is like that" to help solve problems. Includes metaphors, similes and analogies.

**analogies**. A specific comparison between entities. A helpful way to solve problems is to remember a similar (analogous) situation and its outcome. Metaphors are broader, similes more specific.

**analytical intelligence**. One of Sternberg's three kinds of intelligence (Triarchic Theory of Intelligence, along with creative and practical. Analytical intelligence is the ability to compare, contrast, judge, explain and make critical arguments.

**anchor**. A number (typically a price) we use to compare other incoming information. A manufacturer's suggested retail price anchors you at a higher perceived value, making the actual retail price seem like a good deal.

**anecdotal evidence**. Examples based on personal experience of you, those you who, or those you've heard of. Unreliable predictors because of small sample size and uncontrolled conditions. Uncle Charles smoked six cigars a day and lived to be 104.

**animal research**. Using non-humans as research subjects. The disadvantage is that the animals aren't given consent. The advantages are that risky procedures such as heart surgery and be tested on animals before using them on humans. Some studies require autopsies, raising ethical concerns for some.

**animistic thinking**. Occurs in Piaget's preoperational stage, where dolls have feelings too.

**antecedent condition**. The context which precedes a behavior. The circumstances that indicate when to respond (stop light, etc.)

**antecedent**. The stimulus or event that happens before a behavior.

**anterograde amnesia**. Damage to both hippocampi which impacts the ability to form to memories.

**anticipation**. The emotion of expectation, prediction, pleasure, and musical timing.

**anticipatory anxiety**. Worry about something in the past reoccurring. Worried it will happen again. If failed in the past, you anticipate that you will fail in new projects too. For Frankl, we get so afraid of getting symptoms, we get symptoms.

**anxiety**. A combination of uncertainty, fear and uneasiness. One of the primary reasons people see psychologists.

**applied behavior analysis** (ABA). An application of behaviorism to real life. Also called behavior modification. Begins with describing the functional relationship between a behavior and the environment within which it occurs. Then the rewards are systematically manipulated to change a targeted behavior.

**applied research**. In contrast to basic research. Focus is on the application of theory to practical situations.

**approach gradient**. For Dollard & Miller, the closer you get to a reward the better it looks.

**approach**. For Dollard & Miller, movement toward a goal. Like rats, when we want something we move closer, physically or emotionally.

**approach-approach conflict**. For Dollard & Miller, a conflict between two things you don't like or don't want to do.

**approach-avoidance conflict**. For Dollard & Miller, a conflict where a situation has both good and bad things about it.

**Ariely, Dan**. Cognitive psychologist and behavioral economist. Best known for his book Predictably Irrational, and for his description of the IKEA effect, a type of effort cognitive bias.

**Aristotle** (384-322 BC). Sometimes called the first psychologist, Aristotle proposed 3 laws of association (i.e., similarity, contiguity, and opposites). A student of Plato, much of philosophy can be traced by to his writings. He came to Plato as a student but stayed on as a teacher until Plato's death. He served as counselor to Hermias and, later, as tutor to Alexander the Great.

He started a school (the Lyceum), wrote Athens' constitution, and impacted zoology, psychology, ethics, logic, and theology. Aristotle's belief that heavier objects fall faster than lighter ones lasted until Galileo. His view that earth is the center of the universe went unchallenged until Capernicus.

Aristotle argued for the existence of a divine principle above all the rest; the Prime Mover (first cause) was pure intellect, perfect unity and unchangeable. Like Hippocrates, Aristotle noted four basic elements, each with its own "specific gravity." But in addition to earth, air, fire and water, Aristotle added a fifth: ether (to describe the content of the heavens).

**Aristotle's laws of association**. The three laws are similarity (like each other), contiguity (close to or touching each other), and opposites (drastically unlike each other).

**assimilation**. For Piaget, adding of new information to a schema category. In a card catalog it would be adding material to the current card. In contrast to accommodation (adding new categories).

**associated pairs**. Paired associates were first studied by Mary Whiton Calkins. Use pairs of words, she showed that the greatest influence on memory was number of presentations, followed by vividness, followed by recency. Her research led Jung and others to use word associations.

**associated reflex**. Vladimire M Bekhterev's term for classical conditioning. We use Pavlov's terms but Bekhterev's ideas.

**association**. A connection or link between people, ideas or stimuli. In behaviorism, the hypothetical bond between stimulus and response. Although the term was used as an explanation of learning by Aristotle. Wundt and Watson also used the term but there is no agreement on its precise definition or its relative importance.

**associationism**. The predecessor to behaviorism. Starting with Aristotle but including Thorndike and Guthrie, belief that behavior can be explained by associations between stimuli.

**assumptions**. Theoretical presets and declarative statements, often not explicitly stated.

**atheoretical**. Research that is not driven by a theory. Skinner claimed to be atheoretical.

**attention span**. The amount of time people spend on a single task without distracting themselves. The ability to focus attention. For most people, attention span is about 15 minutes.

**attention**. What our mental channel is currently tuned to. Tangen summarizes it as FAR: focus, avoidance and reduction. Titchener summarizes it as involuntary, secondary (voluntary) and derived (habituation).

**attentional bias**. The tendency to pay attention to emotional stimuli or recurring thoughts. When we frequently think about the car we drive, we pay more attention to the cars other people drive.

**attitudes**. Generalized opinions, often expressed nonverbally in posture and micro-movements.

**attribute substitution**. The use of a simple heuristic instead of doing complication computations. The tendency to avoid mental work by substituting catch phrases or simple solutions. "To lose weight, just eat less."

**attribution of causality**. The mental determination of what caused a current state or situation. Often related to correlations.

**auditory encoding**. Extracting meaning from spoken word, music and sounds.

**autism**. A neurodevelopmental disorder whose symptoms appear at about age two and is diagnosed at about three years old. Tends to run in families but no single cause has been identified. A spectrum of symptoms is seen, not everyone gets all the symptoms. It is a complex disorder with several subgroups, including Asperger syndrome. Rett syndrome (which primarily affect girls) is sometimes included.

Some children start off with symptoms and others seem to have normal development but then regress. Much more common in boys than girls. Symptoms include social deficits, resistant to change, limited focus, self-injury, and repetitive behaviors (stacking objects, everything must be lined up). Some have limited or no language ability.

**autobiographical memory**. A type of declarative memory; explicit (not implicit). Long-term personal memory of places, times and events. Also called episodic memory.

**automatic processing**. Cognition is thought to be composed of two types of processing: automatic and controlled. An automatic process doesn't require general processing be devoted to it.

**automatization**. A form of habituation. Going from nervously driving a car as a beginner to performing the tasks smoothly and without seeming to think about it.

**auto-reinforcement**. Anything you do that is rewarding to you, without the need for external reinforcement.

**auto-shaping**. Pigeons repeatedly given short exposure (5 seconds) to a conditioned stimulus (white circle) followed by an unconditioned stimulus (grain) seem to randomly discover the grain and then learn to respond to the white circle. Raises the issue whether the association classical or operant conditioning. Seen in pigeons; not clear how much it generalized.

**auto-stimulation**. Rats with probes inserted into limbic system, repeatedly pushed the level to get more stimulation to that region.

**availability heuristic**. Also known as the availability bias. A cognitive bias that assumes if we can recall it, it must be true. A cognitive bias. When we focus on our past success, we tend to overestimate our future performance. We remember the wins and ignore the losses. More generally, if you can remember it (available), it is important or true.

**availability of strategies**. How many strategies you have to choose between, and how quickly you can access them.

**available memory**. Available suggests it is in there somewhere. Accessible means you can find it. The difference between available and accessible memory is thought to be retrieval errors. Memories that are stored are said to be available. But if cannot find them, they are not accessible. Think of a stuffed, messy tool shed which holds all of your tools. You know there is hammer in there somewhere but it is not easily accessible. It is easier to borrow one from your neighbor than search through your shed.

**aversive conditioning**. Avoidance learning from punishment. Example: putting bitter substance on nails to discourage nail biting or using Antabuse to stop drinking alcohol. Has more side effects and is less effective than positive reinforcement.

**avoid flow**. When you are using interleafed practice, the sensation of flow (everything going easily) is a signal to change to another learning activity.

**avoid**. Our natural tendency to limit our cognitive load. We want to do the least amount of work needed to achieve acceptable results.

**avoidance gradient**. For Dollard & Miller, the closer you get to something you don't like the slower you go.

**avoidance**. The tendency to stay away from painful or unpleasant stimuli.

**avoidance-avoidance conflict**. For Dollard & Miller, a choice between two things don't want. Avoid deciding as long as possible. For rats in shuttle box with shock on both sizes of divider, try to stay in the air as much as possible.

**awfulization**. For Ellis, a type of catastrophic thinking. You stubbed your toe and now it is a complete disaster: you'll probably lose your job and be homeless.

B

**Baby Tender crib**. A crib Skinner made for his daughter. Glass sides to see out, air conditioned for comfort, rolling cloth bottom for easy cleaning. Never caught on; looked too much like an aquarium.

**backward chaining**. An effective mnemonic for learning speeches, songs and long passages text. Also used to train dogs and teach children with developmental issues how to dress themselves. Begin the with last item you want performed, then add to the beginning of the chain. The 12 Days of Christmas is a good example.

**backward conditioning**. In classical conditioning, backward conditioning presents the food before the bell. Not as quickly learned as forward conditioning (bell before food) but common in real life situations.

**Baddeley, Alan**. British memory research who developed a widely used model of working memory.

**balancing skill**. There is no general skill of balance. Each activity requiring balance must be learned separately.

**Bandura, Albert**. Born in 1925 in Mundara, Alberta (Canada), educated in America. Like Tolman, Bandura stressed social learning. He held that behavior is a function of cognitive and environmental factors, and how they interact with previous behaviors. Essentially, environment is what we make it to be. It is our perception of reality.

In addition to classical and operant conditioning, we can learn by observing others (modeling). According to Bandura, we can benefit from other's mistakes, and are motivated by our own goals and dreams. He maintained that people are capable of self-reinforcement (e.g., exceeding your personal standards of performance) and delayed self-gratification. Bandura offers a positive view of people actively involved in real life. Although uncomfortable labeling himself as a cognitive behaviorist, he certainly accepts a softer view of behaviorism.

**bandwagon effect**. A cognitive bias where you base your behavior on what others are doing. If everyone is jumping off the cliff, you go too.

**Barnum effect** (Forer effect). Tendency to rate vague descriptions of personality as highly accurate if you believe they were generated specifically for you. A type of subjective validation.

**Bartlett, Frederic** (1886-1969). British psychologist at University of Cambridge. Best known for War of Ghosts experiments, showing the reconstructive aspects of memory and how we change information to fit our schemas.

**basal ganglia**. Inhibits behavior until activated. The brake system of the brain. Aids learning skills by what it doesn't inhibit.

**basic research**. In contrast to applied research. Focus is on the developing a theory without practical application.

**bearing cognitive map**. Also called vector-based cognitive maps. Instead of landmarks, navigation is done by bearings and coordinates (head this direction for this amount of time).

**Beck, Aaron** (1921-). He combined Rogers and Freud to create Cognitive Therapy. From Rogers, he takes the importance of developing a relationship with the client, and Roger's emphasis on how you see the world (phenomenology).

From Freud, Beck takes the importance of treating severe conditions, the value of a good medical education (Beck got his MD from Yale), and the great impact that internal processing has on external behavior. But instead of Freudian conflicts, the heart of Beck's approach is the impact of beliefs on behavior.

What we believe impacts what we do. Just as our perceptual processes can be distorted, our thinking can be biased. If we have an internal representation of ourselves as hopeless or unlovable, that cognitive bias will impact our behavior. We can make ourselves miserable by over-generalizing a bad day as all life being bad. We might magnify a small issue into a big issue, make everything all about us, or jump to conclusions before we have any evidence. All of these are problems of thinking.

Beck's approach, then, is to fix behavior by fixing the thinking and its underlying assumptions. These assumptions are called schemas. They are assumptions about how the world operates. We generate rules about ourselves, other people, and the world in general. We decide whether we are good, whether others can be trusted, and whether the world is neutral, on our side or against us. Some of these schemas are very general but many are specific to our experience and unique to us. We might have a general rule of life (be kind to others) and a very specific rule of how to act at home (never ask for advice from your mother unless you want to be criticized).

Schema and values are interchangeable. Values that are at the center of who we are. Think of them as super-schema or super-rules. A schema influences some behavior but values influence a lot of behaviors. If these core values are healthy, they are beneficial to us. But if our core beliefs are based on distortions of reality, we will systematically make errors of reasoning throughout our lives. If our belief is that we are incapable of making good decisions, this cognitive bias will result in our being indecisive. Similarly, if we believe we are incompetent, we might expect failure and try to get other people to run our lives for us. If we believe we can't make it through life without help, we might over-value our relationships. Alternatively, if we believe we must make it on our own, we might underestimate the value of intimacy.

The good news is that our personality is not fixed. For Beck, we are what we think. We construct our view of the world from our past experiences and internal processes. If our past twists our thinking, our challenge is to untwist it. Since our thinking causes a lot of our misery, we can make our lives better by examining our assumptions, testing reality and straightening out our thinking.

Despite his emphasis of cognition, Beck is surprisingly behavior oriented. In therapy, clients are taught to specify their behaviors, track them, and modify them. For Beck, thinking and doing are closely tied. Systematic cognitive distortions don't really matter if they don't show up in behavior. And teaching people to identify their dichotomous thinking (it has to be this or that; nothing in between) is of little value unless it produces a change of behavior. For Beck, it's a thinking-doing combo.

**behavior analysis**. Identifying which behaviors are actually occurring. A major focus of behavior modification and applied behavior analysis.

**behavior chain**. A series of behaviors linked together. Chains are either forward or backward chained.

**behavior modification**. A general term for applying conditioning principles to changing behavior, including desensitization (incompatible responses), tokens (reinforcement) and punishment. Based on theories of Thorndike, Pavlov, Skinner and Guthrie.

**behavior potential**. Rotter's belief that behavior is a function of likelihood and reward size. Behavioral potential (BP) is the probability of a behavior occurring. And it is a function of expectations (E) and reinforcement value (RV).

**behavior repertoire**. Mental list of options could do, often filtered by what can do within current circumstances.

**behavior replication**. Skinner's focus was on replicating experimental results, not using statistics or modeling. He believed general principles will be discovered when behaviors can be replicated.

**behavior variability**. It is rare for the same behavior to consistently occur, even under identical circumstances. We think of ourselves as being consistent but our actual behavior varies considerable from day to day.

**behavior**. Everything you do. For Rogers, it is a goal-directed attempt to meet its needs as it perceives them.

**behavioral change**. A combination of Behavior Modification and Applied Behavioral Analysis. A general term for applying conditioning principles to changing behavior, including desensitization (incompatible responses), tokens (reinforcement) and punishment. Based on theories of Thorndike, Pavlov, Skinner and Guthrie.

**behavioral potential** (BP). Rotter's model of predicting behavior (behavioral potential) is a combination of the likelihood of a reward and the size of the reward.

**behavioral therapy**. Beck's approach has three steps: identify maladaptive behaviors, remove them, and substitute more adaptive and appropriate behaviors. There is no need to review the individual's past or encourage them to relive it. Change is not dependent on self-understanding or insight.

**behaviorism**. The second force of psychology. A reaction to psychoanalysis, behaviorism hypothesized to internal processes (black box). All behavior could be explained by stimulus (input) and response (output). The second wave of psychology. A reaction to psychoanalysis. The emphasis is on observable behaviors, not intrapsychic and unconscious motivations.

**behaviors**. According to Tangen, one of the three things that can be learned. Behaviors are anything you do, anything that can be made into a verb and anything that must be practiced.

**Bekhterev, Vladimire** (1857-1927). A contemporary of Pavlov, Bechterev gave a more psychological interpretation of classical conditioning. His "associated reflex" described the process better but Pavlov's terms prevailed. Bechterev began the first experimental psychology lab in Russia (at the University of Kazan). Following his graduation, Bekhterev studied with Wundt, DeBois-Reymond and Charcot.

Instead of Pavlov's conditioned reflex, Bechterev called it an "associated reflex." Instead of studying secretions (a very physiological orientation), Bechterev studied motor reflexes.

For Bechterev, behavior was completely explainable within a S-R (stimulus-response) format. Psychology was for him simply "human reflexology."

**belief bias**. Strength of belief is interpreted as truth. The stronger we believe something the more logical and true it is.

**belief**. In cognitive behavioral theory, an assumption about oneself or others that filters the input (activating event) and leads to an outcome (feeling). Beliefs are personal opinions which we accept as being true. A belief can be shared by an entire group or be the sole possession of one person. As opinions, beliefs often are untestable statements of faith.

**bias**. Prejudice or tendency to think a particular way. Also called cognitive bias.

**big G**. According to Spearman, general intelligence. It is difficult to directly measure.

**binding problem**. How to get consciousness from neurons. Part of the mind-body problem.

**black box**. The analogy that the mind is like a black box, no one knows what is going on inside. Behaviorists used the analogy to suggest that only inputs and outputs can be studied.

**blank slate**. Locke's proposal that we are born without innate ideas. Our minds are a blank slate (tabula rasa).

**blocked goals**. For Dollard & Miller, aggression is caused by blocked goals. A rat in a blocked tunnel that used to be open will try to climb it or scratch and bite at it. In humans, getting cut off in traffic is a blocked goal.

**blocked practice**. Also called normal practice. We tend to learn task A, then move on to task B. Blocked practice is good for short-term learning. Interleafed practice (some time on A, some time on B, sometime of A) is better for long-term learning.

**blocking**. Putting similar items together. TV news shows put all the sports stories together in a block. Similarly, they block the weather stories, traffic reports and kitten videos.

**Bobo the Clown**. An inflatable, egg-shaped punching bag used by Bandura to study aggression. Film of person punching the clown, shouting "sockeroo!" is shown to kindergartners. In play time, children show increased aggression. Boys were generally more violent and aggressive than girls. Video or film worked equally well as human models.

**body language**. The inexact art of predicting internal states from external gestures, postures and expressions.

**bond size**. Tangen's way of explaining the difference in approaches of Pavlov-Thorndike and Guthrie to stimulus-response bonds. Pavlov and Thorndike thought of S-R bonds as being large connections. But Guthrie maintained the connections are made at the movement level, where many millions of tiny s-r connections are made.

**bonds**. A basic part of behaviorism. Learning is thought of as forming connections between stimuli and responses. Bonds tend to be unidirectional (one way only).

**bottom-up processing**. The opposite of top-down processing (evaluating incoming stimuli as words or music). Bottom-up processing gathers all of the bits together and figures out the puzzle.

**bounded rationality**. Herbert Simon's term which indicates that there are limits to what we know. What your competitor is doing is outside the bounds of your rationality. Decisions are always made with limited knowledge.

**BP = $f$(E & RV)**. Rotter's formula for choosing a behavior. Behavior is a function of likelihood and reward size. Behavioral potential (BP) is the probability of a behavior occurring. And it is a function of expectations (E) and reinforcement value (RV).

This formula predicts behavior, and consequently is a guide of how to conduct therapy. For Rotter, symptoms are learned, so therapy should be a learning situation. The focus of therapy can be on any component in Rotter's model. The first source of trouble might be a client's behavior (BP). Neurotic behavior might simply be maladaptive itself and need to be changed. Neurotic behavior also can be caused by unrealistic expectations (E). The cure for this condition is to explore why the client sets expectations so high or so low.

People tend to have a minimal goal: a hallmark of success and failure. Achieving less than the minimal goal would be considered failing, even if the minimal goal had been set unrealistically high.

RV is reinforcement value. Here is the recognition that systematically over- or under-valuing rewards can lead to trouble. Corrective therapy might focus on the nature and size of desired rewards. Clients might examine why it is not enough for them when people say that they look good.

**brain as a fist**. An easy way to explain the brain to kids. The thumb is the temporal lobe, the front edge is the frontal lobe, the knuckles represents the parietal lobe, and the back of the hand is the occipital lobe.

**brain damage**. Structure damage to the cells of the cerebrum causing functional difficulty. Common causes are traumatic injury (car crashes, football, boxing, soccer), developmental disorders and drugs.

**brain plasticity** (neuroplasticity). The ability of the brain to reprogram itself to new experiences. The brain has more plasticity during youth and less as you age.

**brainstorming**. The process of generating ideas and options. Best done without evaluating the ideas as they are being generated.

**Bransford & Johnson**. Best known for their study of schema, using a paragraph about balloons, music and serenading a woman. Subject given a picture indicating how the items fit together understand and remember the passage better than those given only the paragraph. This serenade experiment shows that context before learning helps but doesn't help after.

**breadth-first search**. In contrast to depth-first, a breadth-first search looks at all the branches at the same level before going further down the tree.

**breaking habits**. The best way to break a habit it to replace it with an incompatible response. For more, see Guthrie's FITS.

**Brewer & Treyens**. Best known for their 1981 study called the Waiting Room Study. Subjects wait in room for less than a minute are asked to list the objects that were in the office. Subjects listed items that would be in an office but were not in that office (books, etc.). Shows evidence of schemas being using in incidental learning situations.

**bridging stimulus**. In animal training, a cue that is given to precisely state when a desired behavior is done. Verbal bridging stimuli are common (good, great, yes) and clickers (with a mechanical snap or electronic tone) usually work better. Clickers aren't used in other areas of life, provide a short cue, have a distinctive sound, and are only used for training.

**Bruner, Jerome** (1915-). A pioneer in cognitive, developmental and educational psychology. Coined the term "scaffolding" to describe that we build on our previous knowledge. Advocated a spiral curriculum, come back around to the topics in more detail, adding to the scaffolded structure. Showed our internal interpretations affect our perceptions: poor kids overestimate the size of coins but not similar size objects. The importance of the money makes them look bigger. Suggested we code things (mentally represent them) by how they look (iconic representation), what they do (action representation) or by language (symbolic representation).

**buffers**. Sensory information is temporarily put in a fairly rapidly-refreshed memory store. Iconic memory is a sensory buffer for visual information that lasts about ½ second. Echoic memory is a sensory buffer for auditory information that lasts 3-4 seconds.

# C

**Cabrera, Derek**. System theorist who proposes four universal structuring factors (skills) he calls DSPR: distinctions, systems, relationships, and perspectives.

**Calkins, Mary**. First to study word associations. Showed that frequency has more impact than vividness, which has more impact than recency. First woman president of the American Psychological Association.

**calming signals**. Dog trainer Turid Rugaas (Norwegian) describes 30+ signals dogs give each other. Allows you to look for subtle signs that your dog is or isn't stressed.

**categorical variables**. Nominal level of measurement uses numbers to indicate categories (tall, medium, short). Includes dichotomous variables (yes or no).

**categories**. Grouping of words or ideas by similarity. Recalling using categories is easier than not, even if no categories were provided to you.

**categorization**. The process of sorting items into categorical buckets.

**causal attribution**. Although correlations indicate strength and direction of relationship, causation must be inferred, regardless of the research design.

**causal modeling**. An abstract model used to represent complex psychological theories. Quantitative data is combined into factors and their interrelationships described.

**causality**. The principle of cause and effect; the reason things occur. One of Hume's 3 laws of association.

**cause-effect**. In contrast to correlation, evidence that an independent variable affects a dependent variable. A causes B but B does not cause A.

**central executive**. Executive processor. Similar to Aristotle's common sense (one that coordinates all senses). The cognitive process of switching from one task to another. The ability to coordinate mental activities.

**centration**. During Piaget's preoperational stage, children are able to focus only on one aspect or characteristic at a time. Once a salient factor is found, it is difficult for young children to switch to another factor.

**cerebellum**. Needed to learn motor skills. Excitatory effects are balanced by the inhibitory effect of the basal ganglia.

**cerebrum**. The combination of the cerebral cortex and its substructure, including the hippocampus and, basal ganglia.

**chaining of thoughts**. Thoughts can trigger each other. Repetitive chains of disturbing thoughts can be difficult to break. Thought stopping is a controversial technique used to interrupt chains of thoughts. Other techniques seem to work better.

**chains of movements**. Behaviors can be chained together, either forward or backward. Forward chaining is typically how we learn a song or story. We start at the beginning and add additional information as we go. Backward chaining is often more effective but less used. Start with the last line of a speech or the last behavior in a chain (sit). Then add links to the front of the chain (middle of the speech or getting the paper off the porch).

**chance**. The assumption that variables in the universe are symmetrically bell-shaped. The null hypothesis is that differences observed are due to chance.

**characteristics of a theory**. Tangen's model suggests that there are six qualities of a good theory (CUSS IT): clear, useful, summarizes facts, small number of assumptions, internally consistent and testable hypotheses.

**Chase & Simon**. Best known for their 1973 study of chess experts. They estimated expert chess players have a vocabulary of up to 50,000 patterns. These patterns represent familiar configurations of chess pieces.

**child-directed speech** (CDS). Cross-culturally, adults adjust their speech when speaking to little children. The sentences are shorter, tone is higher, the words exaggerated and the pronunciation clear. Children prefer CDS and it helps them learn language faster.

**childhood amnesia** (infantile amnesia). Inability to remember anything before age 2-4, varying with the person. Believed to be the result of the brain's not having fully developed a linguistic encoding system and storage.

**childhood memories**. Hazy, clear and inaccurate memories from when we are young. Tend to remember pictures of childhood events better.

**choice**. Usually divided into rational choice theory and other types. Rational choice suggests people weigh options before deciding. Other theories, including Ariely's predicable irrationality suggest we are greatly impacted by cognitive biases.

**chunking**. The naïve mnemonic of breaking a long sequence into smaller segments. Shown in our perceptual system by items close together being groups together. Chunks contain 3-4 items or 3-4 chunks of items.

**circular logic**. A practical logical fallacy whose premises and conclusions are equally untested. The fallacy is easy to catch in short statement but difficult in long chains of reasoning. The famous "Wellington is in New Zealand; therefore, Wellington is in New Zealand." Or "You are a sinner because you sin. You sin because you're a sinner."

**classical conditioning**. According to Pavlov, learning is a function of preceding bonds between stimuli. Once conditioned a stimulus will elicit a response from the animal. Conditioning is the repeated presentation of stimuli.

**classification**. A cognitive process involved in perception, decision making and adaptation. Grouping items into categories requires perception, differentiation, object recognition and decision making.

**clear**. One of Tangen's CUSSIT criteria for testing a theory. Clear theories are better than vague theories.

**Clever Hans**. A horse whose trainer (Wilheim van Osten) believed could add, subtract, multiple, read and do other intellectual feats. The horse was able to perform these tricks in single-blind conditions but not in double-blind conditions. Hans watched the body language of the observers.

**clicker training**. Mostly used in animal training and high performance sports. Uses a clicker to indicate that a specific behavior was correct.

**clicker**. Mechanical or electronic device that makes a click. Used to signal the correct response in human and animal training. Allows trainer-coach to be further away yet deliver a precise marker signal.

**closed environment** (problem solving). A problem space with limits movements and options. A well-defined problem. Predictable, limited changes in the environment. Movements can be planned in advance. Includes chess, gymnastics, figure skating and classical music.

**clustering**. Both informal (put similar items together) and formal multivariate cluster analysis are used to identify commonality between ideas.

**Cocktail Party effect**. Broadbent's study on our ability to listen to one conversation with one ear and another one with the other. Shows the limits of human attention.

**coding**. Converting information to a more easily stored format. Includes meaning extraction.

**cognition**. The multidisciplinary study of thinking, memory, attention, language and decision making.

**cognitive artifacts**. Objects (physical or virtual) that aid learning by reducing memory loads. Examples include, checklists, graphs, infographics, and objects (such as Tinkertoys for modeling organic molecules). Artifacts help display information, simplify steps and reduce errors.

**cognitive behaviorism**. The theoretical approach proposed by Edward Tolman.

**cognitive bias**. Systematic reasoning patterns that are useful heuristics that are based on how our perceptual systems work. Biases include positivism, fundamental attribution error, free is always better, belief bias and confirmation bias.

**cognitive development**. The growth of thinking, problem solving and decision making. The development of the mind.

**cognitive distortions**. For Beck, exaggerated or inaccurate thoughts and beliefs. More generally, turning thingamabobs into things in a box.

**cognitive domain**. The multidimensional approach to development is composed of three domains: biosocial, cognitive and psychosocial. The focus is on mental processes. Topics include knowledge, awareness, sensation, perception, language and memory.

**cognitive load**. The brain can't handle everything at once. The more tasks it is given to perform simultaneously, the great the cognitive load.

**cognitive maps**. Mental representations of spatial information. Tasks include finding your way through a maze or finding your way back home. The hippocampus and surrounding regions generate two types: vector (coordinates) and sketch (landmarks. Some people prefer one over the other.

**cognitive miser**. Once we have accepted a value, conclusion or stereotype, we are resistant to change. We are not willing to spend the cognitive effort to question our assumptions.

**cognitive neuroscience approach**. The study of the biological structures and processes in the brain that make thinking possible.

**cognitive process**. A construct that depicts thinking as a subroutine or divides cognition into knowledge, attention, etc.

**cognitive rule**. The brain's tendency to ignore steady-state information.

**cognitive schema**. Mental representations of how the world works. Build up by experience and influenced by culture.

**cognitive self-regulation**. A metacognitive rule that monitors and controls an individual, particularly in the selection of alternative processes or strategies. An executive process.

**cognitive structures**. Theoretical assumption that ideas are formed into structures and mental representations.

**cognitive theory**. Any theory how the mind develops and functions, including those by Aristotle, Piaget and neuroscience.

**cognitive triad**. For Beck, the negative thoughts are about three things: ourselves, the world and the future. We think of ourselves as worthless, assume the world is unfair and believe the future is bleak.

**cognitive**. An adjective describing thinking, will or intellect; as opposed to conative (emotional).

**cognitive-affective complexity**. Thinking and emotions are intertwined. As people mature the interactions between these systems become more complex.

**cognitive-developmental theory**. Any theory that describes the development of the mind and how thinking changes in children.

**collections of movements**. For Guthrie, tiny micromovements are combined into collections called acts.

**color, size, shape, bold, underlying**…. Variations that make text more memorable.

**competence**. Confidence proceeds competence. We become competent (able to perform a skill) after we are confident we can do it. We must practice beyond confidence.

**complete memory**. Ebbinghaus' term for remembering a list completely one time.

**complex environment**. A combination of open and closed environments. A standup comic, for example, plan joke sequence but must adjust to hecklers and improvisations.

**complex skills**. A combination of simple skills. Requires timing and coordination. Includes changing gears in a stick shift, twirling a Hula-Hoop on each arm, a lay-up (instead of a free-throw), etc.

**conative**. Emotional, not cognitive. A natural tendency or impulse.

**concept map**. A graphic description of concepts and their relationship to each other. Like a mind map with no center prompt.

**concepts**. According to Tangen, one of the three things that can be learned. Concepts must be illustrated.

**concrete operational stage**. For Piaget, the third stage of cognitive development; occurs between 7 and 12. Children are able to begin thinking like a scientist but can't use abstract concepts or symbols. Reasoning is logical but based on what can be seen. Can't do hypotheticals.

**concrete operations** (concrete thinking). According to Piaget, the ability to perform abstract thinking (formal operations) is preceded by a stage of reasoning (ages 7-12) which is limited to classifying objects, manipulating numbers; conservation is acquired during this period but those at this stage of development are unable to discuss hypothetical situations.

**conditioned response** (CR). In Pavlov's studies, the conditioned response is salivating to the bell. Similar but not as strong a response as an UCR. According to Pavlov, the response to a stimulus which has been previously paired with a stimulus which evokes a response; the conditioned response is similar to the unconditioned response but is lower in magnitude. Pavlov called it "psychic secretion."

**conditioned stimulus** (CS). In Pavlov's studies, the CS is the bell. According to Pavlov, when a neutral stimulus is paired with a stimulus which evokes a response, the previously neutral stimulus (the conditioned stimulus) evokes a similar but weaker response.

**conditioning inhibition**. More difficult to classically condition to a familiar or commonly encountered conditioned stimulus.

**conditioning**. A general term for behaviorist learning. Has been applied to Thorndike, Guthrie, Pavlov and Skinner. Usually divided into connectionism (Thorndike), all-or-none learning (Guthrie), classical conditioning (Pavlov) and operant conditioning (Skinner).

**confabulation**. Memory disorder. Recalling facts that didn't happen. Common in childhood memories and in Korsakoff's syndrome.

**confidence precedes competence**. We overestimate our ability to perform before we are able to actually do a task.

**confidence**. Confidence proceeds competence. We become confident of our knowledge or skill before we are actually able to perform it reliably.

**confirmation bias**. After we buy something we love it more. We tend to only look at evidence that supports our decision. Search for supporting data to reduce inconsistency.

**conflict**. A fight or battle between opposing forces, needs or desires. For Freud, conflict can be unconscious.
For Lewin (and later, Dollard and Miller's studies), there are four types of conflict: approach-approach conflicts are

between two desirable choices; approach-avoidance conflicts are the result of an option which is both desirable and undesirable; avoidance-avoidance is the choice between to undesirable states.

**consequence**. In cognitive behavioral theory, a feeling which is a result of an activating event being filtered by a belief.

**conservation**. For Piaget, children in the concrete stage learn that objects are the same when presented in different orientations. Eight ounces in a small cup is the same as eight ounces in a large cup (conservation of volume). There are the same number of square if they are spaced out or tightly grouped (conservation of area). Pencils don't get larger if you move one over (conservation of length). A rolled up and an unrolled candy weigh the same amount (conservation of weight). Conservation is the ability to judge quantity regardless of shape (e.g., narrow tall glass holds same as short wide glass).

**consolidation**. Process of converting short-term memories to long-term memories. Hippocampus is critical for consolidating long-term memories but not for recalling them. For Mahler, stage four of individuation is the unification of the good and bad mother. The start of a child's own individuality coincides with their superstation (going to personhood). The child develops a self-concept based on a stable sense of "me." This occurs from 24-36 months of age.

**constructive alternativism**. For Kelly, if your constructs aren't working for you, choose an alternative one.

**constructivist classroom**. An approach to education that puts the focus on the student "constructing" their own constructs. Typically, there are less lectures, more tasks and varying amounts of self-directed learning.

**constructs**. Ideas. The components of a theory Theories are composed of constructs; models are composed of variables. Used as theoretical building blocks to form theories, constructs are ideas. By systematically arranging ideas, a complex pattern of concepts can be developed. This pattern (theory), though often untestable, relates observable and abstract elements together in interesting ways.

**context analysis**. A stimulus occurs within a context. Context analysis tries to identify all of the environmental cues that might impact a stimulus. State- and location-dependent cues are part of the context.

**context**. The environment within which a stimulus is presented.

**context-dependent cues**. Environmental cues used to help encode information, including where you are and who you are with.

**context-dependent memory**. Easier to remember in the learning environment you learned in. Remembering a thought in the kitchen but not in the living room is the result of context-dependent cues.

**contextual distinctiveness**. Also called primary distinctiveness. One aspect stands out compared to the context. The von Restroff effect is the result of printing a word in a different color in the middle of a list; make the word easier to remember and makes the whole list easier to remember.

**contiguity**. A series of adjacent elements; connected by time, placement or relationship. One of Aristotle's laws of association (similarity, contiguity and opposites). One of Hume's 3 laws of association (contiguity, resemblance and causality). A Gestalt principle used to organize perceptions (things close to each other); for Erickson, the continuity of past, present and future is an important consideration.

**contiguous associations**. For Aristotle, things that are close in time or space are associated together.

**contingency**. Must do X to get Y.

**continuity**. A Gestalt principle used to organize perceptions (things close to each other); for Erickson, the continuity of past, present and future is an important consideration

**continuous movement**. As opposed to discreet movement. Any flowing motion. Peddling a bicycle, drawing circles, dancing, walking or running. Any movement that cannot be described as either-or or on-off. Smooth cyclical movements with no clear beginning or end. Includes skating a figure 8, swimming, cycling and steering a car.

**continuous schedule of reinforcement**. Get rewarded every time you do a given behavior. Primarily used to teach and shape a behavior.

**continuous**. In contrast to discrete. Continuous variables are used in correlation. Discrete variables are used in categorization. For developmental changes, stages can be gradual waves (continuous) or discrete steps (set stages).

**control processes**. The subroutines of the executive process, including synthesizing inputs, selection of alternatives and analyzing patterns. Perhaps these processes get worse as we age.

**controls** (control group). In an experiment, subjects who do not receive the experimental treatment.

**convergent thinking**. In contrast to divergent thinking. Using multiple points of view to solve problems. Being rewarded to finding interconnection.

**coping strategies**. For Horney, there are three types of neurotic coping strategies: moving toward (compliance), moving against (hostility) and moving away (detachment).

**core irrational beliefs**. Basic assumptions, untested in reality. Include "I am a loser," "I can't do anything," and "There is no way I can fail."

**Cornell note-taking system**. Notes are taken in the main section (right 2/3$^{rd}$ of a page) in outline form. Afterwards, or when it pops into your head, questions are put in the left 1/3$^{rd}$ section of the page. At the bottom of the page (or the end of the notes), a paraphrase summary of the important ideas is written. This system is particularly helpful as a reminder that processing your notes is as important as taking them.

**correction**. Another term for punishment, as in a correctional institution.

**correlation coefficient**. A numerical description of relationship. Values can range from +1 to -1. The sign (positive or negative) indicates the direction of relationship. Magnitude indicates the strength of relationship (stronger the closer to get to 1, either positive or negative).

**correlation**. Originally proposed by Galton as co-relation and displayed in a scatterplot; later Pearson, Spearman and others developed statistical computations for describing monotonic and linear relationship. Values can range from +1 to -1. The sign (positive or negative) indicates the direction of relationship. Magnitude indicates the strength of relationship (stronger the closer to get to 1, either positive or negative).

**correspondence bias**. Also called fundamental attribution error. We fundamentally tend to blame our lateness on external events (slow traffic) but blame the lateness of others on internal characteristics that correspond to their personality.

**cost-benefit analysis**. Also called benefit-cost analysis. Logical comparison of strengths and weakness of alternatives. Similar to cost-effectiveness analysis. How we think we make decisions but often not how we actually make decisions. Process of comparing strengths and weaknesses. Damage to dorsolateral cortex impairs this ability.

**counterconditioning**. Also called stimulus substitution and systematic desensitization. For Mary Cover Jones, calming stimuli occur at same time as anxiety initiating behavior, creating an incompatible response. Earing favorite food while watching a rabbit you're afraid of, petting a dog while it is nervous, or hugging kids during a thunderstorm. The strength of positive stimuli must overwhelm the strength of fearful stimuli. Thought to be more than extinction.

**covert behavior**. Behaviors you can't see, or not easily see.

**covert-unlearned**. Behaviors you can't see, or not easily see, that are innate (reflexes).

**CPR**. Stands for cardiopulmonary resuscitation. Procedures (chest compressions and ventilation) used to restore breathing and blood circulation. A skill which is mostly forgotten within a year.

**cramming**. Massed practice that occurs the night before a big test. Not effective for long-term learning.

**creative intelligence**. One of Sternberg's three kinds of intelligence (Triarchic Theory of Intelligence, along with analytical and practical. Creative intelligence is the ability to have insight, synthesize information and deal with novel situations.

**creativity** Also called divergent thinking. Generating new ideas and finding new interactions between ideas.

**criteria**. Specified outcomes used for comparisons. Behavioral or situational statements used to indicate that you've reached your goal.

**critical period**. Relatively short period of time in which event or experience must occur for normal development. The critical period for binocular vision is 3-8 months after birth. If infants can't use both eyes during this period, they will never develop binocular vision.

**critical thinking**. Also called critical analysis. The basis of the Socratic method of learning. Making reasoned judgments based on logical arguments, examining both sides of the argument.

**cross-maze**. A maze in the shape of a cross or X. Typically used in animal research involving memory and choice.

**cryptomnesia**. Inadvertently stealing another person's song, speech, etc.

**crystallized intelligence**. Also called crystalized thinking. For Cattell, skills and task knowledge. In contrast to fluid intelligence.

**cue**. One of four Dollard and Miller's four units of learning. A stimulus that tell person when, where and how to respond.

**cued recall**. Retrieval based on a specific cue; what was the fourth word, etc.

**cue-dependent forgetting**. Inability to retrieve memories without cues. Can recognize but not recall. Includes semantic, state-dependent and context cues.

**cultural schema**. Rules about what people in your culture do. We play these sports, enjoy this music, have this amount of personal distance, and use these gestures.

**current moment bias**. Prefer current pleasure, leave pain for the future.

**CUSS IT**. Tangen's model suggests that there are six qualities of a good theory: clear, useful, summarizes facts, small number of assumptions, internally consistent and testable hypotheses.

**CVC**. Consonant-vowel-consonant combinations used to make artificial words for studying memory. Used to learn lists, like Ebbinghaus.

# D

**Darwin, Charles** (1809-1882). In response to Alfred Wallace's proposed publication, Darwin published his notes and theory of evolution, causing a major shift in intellectual thought. At the age of 22, just out of college and trying to avoid becoming an ordained minister, Charles Robert Darwin served as an unpaid naturalist on an around the world expedition.

After his trip and his father's death, Darwin retired into the life of a country gentleman. Then, a young naturalist, Alfred Russell Wallace, proposed a theory of natural selection and sent a copy to Darwin. Darwin then wrote his own version, and both were published in 1858. In what could be called the Wallace-Darwin theory of evolution, generational changes in a species are due to their ability to adapt to the environment.

Before Darwin, the world was thought of a series of catastrophes. The last great catastrophic event (Noah's flood) had wiped out all animals except those on the ark. Darwin's speculation that related organisms come from common ancestors brought into question the immutability of species and, by extension, the special creation of humans.

Darwin's theory of evolution replaced Lamarck's contention that the effects of practice could be seen in one's offspring. Instead, one's survival was attributed to the ability to react to environmental changes.

**data structures**. In computer science, ways to organize information. In cognition, the way memories are stored.

**decay theory of forgetting**. The hypothesis that memories fade over time in a linear fashion (a little bit at a time).

**decision complexity**. A function of the number of factors or options in a decision. Think of a nine-page menu as complex and a choice between 3 options as simple. The more options we have the less satisfied we are with the outcome.

**decision fatigue**. The more decisions we make, the less we want to make any decisions.

**decision making**. Choose between options.

**declarative memory**. All of the information you can explain (declare). In contrast to implicit memory.

**decoding**. Retrieving the information from long-term memory and reconstructing memories. Generally, transferring from a sparsely coded state to an elaborated state.

**deductive reasoning**. Top-down thinking or reasoning from general rules to specific instances. This method was favored by Descartes, Galileo, Hobbes and Sherlock Holmes. Based on the assumption that if the premises are true, the conclusion will also be true (if the rules of logic are correctly applied).

**default setting**. Our tendency to some home, flip on the TV without even changing the channel. Generally, acceptance of things as they are, usually as a result of being tired of making decisions.

**deferential analysis**. Choosing between several option by focusing on specific components or characteristics.

**deferred imitation**. The ability to recall & model behavior of a model not there.

**delayed matching-to-sample task**. Used to study declarative memory in animals. Subject must choose the object that matches the sample. Time between stimulus and response opportunity is varied.

**delayed retrieval**. In animal studies, time between showing where something is and allowing the animal to get it. A measure of working memory.

**delayed-response task**. A delay between stimulus and response is imposed to study attention, memory and spatial reasoning.

**deliberate practice**. The type of practice experts use. Practice to solve a problem (fingering, peddles, phrasing, etc.). Not simple repetition.

**deliberative reasoning**. Thoughtful reasoning with carefully stated arguments.

**delusions**. Strongly held but mistaken belief. Not based on false information but a self-created, unjustifiable belief. Common in schizophrenia and manic episodes. Includes thought insertion, bizarre beliefs (controlled by aliens) and paranoia (being spied on).

**demonstrable**. Concrete, rather than abstract. Can be shown, not theoretical.

**depletion**. The lowering of energy that occurs for every decision you make.

**depth-first search**. In contrast to breadth-first, a depth-first search follows on branch down through all its levels before looking at another branch.

**derived attention**. According to Titchener, the habit of attending to a stimulus produces derived attention. In contrast to voluntary attention, derived attention requires less mental effort.

**desensitization**. Diminished response to a stimulus. Can be casual or systematic.

**determinants of unconscious behavior**. For Dollard and Miller, there are factors: unaware of certain drives or cues (a problem of things being unlabeled), and cues or responses that were conscious but have we have learned to ignore (repression).

**developmental stages**. Learning can be described as occurring in stages. These stage may or may not be tied to biological stages of development.

**differential reinforcement of other behavior** (DRO). A form of omission training (training to not do something). Ignore unwanted behavior (head banding) but reward when not doing it.

**differential reinforcement**. The goal is to increase desired behaviors and not reinforce undesired behaviors.

**differentiation**. To make distinctions. The third stage of neural development. Neurons differentiate from other cells by getting axons and dendrites (in that order).

**digestive reflexes**. Pavlov won a Nobel Prize for his work studying digestive reflexes.

**dimension** (up-down). We have little difficulty remembering which dimension was mentioned (vertical or horizontal) but don't remember whether it is up or down.

**discovery learning**. Jerome Bruner popularized inquiry-based learning. Students are not provided an exact answer but are given materials to use acquire information and solve problems.

**discrete movement**. In contrast to continuous movements, discrete actions are nominal (yes-no, on-off. Pressing a key or flipping a switch. Well-defined actions with a clear beginning and a clear ending. Each part is an independent action. Includes typing, pounding nails, hitting balls and flipping a switch.

**discrimination**. In behaviorism, the ability to detect differences between stimuli.

**discriminative stimulus**. A stimulus that indicates what to do or not do. A traffic stop light for humans. A tone or light for animal research.

**disorganized thinking**. A positive symptom (must have) for diagnosing schizophrenia. Thinking is scattered, not linear.

**dissociate fugue**. Also called a psychogenic fugue or fugue state. Probably doesn't exist. In theory, patient loses but recovers memory for everything, including personal identity.

**dissociative amnesia**. No evidence it exists. In theory, patients can't remember (repress) memories of traumatic events.

**distance**. A Dollard & Miller term. When we want something, we physically or emotionally approach it. How far away we are (distance) from an object impacts the stimulus intensity. As we get closer to rewards, the better they look. As we get closer to punishments, the worse they look.

**distinctions**. Characteristics that differ between objects or ideas.

**distinctiveness**. A process of focusing attention. Three major types: primary (von Restroff), secondary (1st time experiences) and emotional (Zeigarnik effect).

**distorted memory**. Memories that have been changed or corrupted after storage, typically by combining them with other information. Once reconsolidated, these distorted or false memories are recognized by the system as true and unchanged.

**distorting effects**. Our tendency to change inputs to match existing schema. An example of how memory is not permanent.

**distractions**. A stimulus purposely or accidently presented which change attentional focus.

**distributed practice**. Also called spaced practice. Learning is spread out over many sessions, each session relatively short. Good for long-term learning.

**divergent thinking**. In contrast to convergent thinking. Taking multiple paths from a single starting point. Being rewarded for creativity.

**divide and conquer**. Strategy of breaking down large problems into solvable segments.

**doctrine of formal discipline**. The position by Locke and others that the best way to train a mind is to teach mathematics, classical literature and foreign languages.

**Dollard & Miller therapy**. The application of Dollard-Miller's psychoanalytic learning theory. Proposed a pragmatic, action oriented, two phase approach. First, in the talking phases, clients learn problem analysis and label identification. Second, in the performance phase, clients acquire new responses to old cues. They are trained in response suppression (conscious, deliberate stopping of a thought or action) and are deliberately exposed to new cues that will evoke different responses.

**Dollard & Miller**. John Dollard & Neal Miller proposed a combination of behaviorism and psychoanalysis. Used animal research to explain conflict. Conflicts include approach-approach, avoidance-avoidance, approach-avoidance and double-approach-avoidance.

**don't forget**. Tangen's general principle that it is easier to keep things in memory than to put them there. Check periodically to see if what you've learned is still there. Use the expanded rehearsal strategy.

**don't punish**. The best approach to changing behavior (yours and others) is to reward behaviors you want increased, and extinguish (ignore) behaviors you want to go away).

**doodling**. Random drawings can aid learning by focusing your attention on your notes while you listen to a lecture.

**dopamine**. A neurotransmitter which signal that an event is important and should be attended to or remembered.

**double approach-avoidance conflict**. For Dollard & Miller, a conflict between two items, each with positive and negative factors. A rat is put in the middle of a maze with food and shock at one end and food and shock at the other. It tends to spend all its time running back and forth without ever reaching the food.

**double-blind study**. The subjects don't know which experimental group they are in (single blind). The people who administer or run the experiment don't know who is in which experimental group (double blind). The people who analyze the results don't know what the study is trying to prove (triple blind).

**draw a picture of the problem situation**. When brainstorming, try switching to a different modality: visual, auditory, spatial, etc.

**dress rehearsal**. Practice session preceding a performance, with every detail present: costumes, lighting, etc. Guthrie recommends more dress rehearsals because all of the cues which impact learning are present.

**drive reduction**. Freud, Hull and others believe that satisfying a drive or reducing its intensity is reinforcing.

**drive, cue, response, reward** (or consequence). The four components of Dollard & Miller's theory.

**drive**. One of four Dollard and Miller's four units of learning. A preexisting need. Can be either a primary or secondary drive. Drives are strong internal stimulus, produces discomfort. They come in two types: primary and secondary. For Rogers, the basic human drive is to be a fully functioning person, who lives by his/her values and not society's/parents' values. The forward push needs have on behavior; psychic energy.

**driving range**. In golf, a place for massed practice: hitting balls as far as you can, one after another.

**drugs**. Three main types are depressants (alcohol, opioids, etc.), stimulants (cocaine, meth, etc.) and hallucinogenics (psychedelics, dissociatives, etc.).

**dry tech rehearsal**. Stage rehearsals with no performers present; lights are turned lights on and off, curtains raised, etc.

**duration**. A length of time; persistence.

**dynamic stereotype**. Pavlov coined the term to describe mental functioning: it is neurologically stable (stereotyped) but responsive to the environment (dynamic).

E

**early selection**. In perception, one of several filter theories. Early selection occurs when a stimulus is selected early in the processing chain. In contrast, late selection occurs when a stimulus is selected late in the processing chain.

**Ebbinghaus, Hermann** (1850-1909). A contemporary of Wundt, Ebbinghaus experimentally studied and described learning, forgetting, overlearning, and savings. His work is widely used and cited by cognitive psychologists today.

Ebbinghaus read Fechner's book (Elements of Psychophysics), which inspired him to study for the mind works. Unaware that Wundt proclaimed it was impossible to study higher mental processes experimentally, Ebbinghaus did so. In 18, at his home in Berlin, Ebbinghaus performed the first experimental work on memory.

Although he was the first person to publish an article on measuring the intelligence of school children (Binet and Simon used his sentence completion task in their intelligence test), Ebbinghaus is best known for his thorough study of memory and forgetting. After creating a list of words to study (each one of a separate card), Ebbinghaus attempted to learn the entire list. Items on each list were kept in order, but since the relationship between the words was arbitrary the lists are said to have been "nonsense" words. Some lists were relearned in order to measure the "savings" on each trial.

Ebbinghaus' famous "retention curve" was a plot of savings as a function of time. Ebbinghaus showed experimentally what people have suspected all along. Forgetting occurs rapidly in the first few hours after learning but it levels out. The best strategy for limiting the decline in recall is to "overlearn" the material (continue studying it after the list can be recalled without error).

**echoic memory**. Buffer for auditory inputs, lasts 3-4 seconds.

**economy of motion**. A measure of skill fluidity (mounting the bars).

**effect**. A noun meaning the outcome of manipulating an independent variable. The consequences of behavior strength (or weaken) the S-R bonds, as in the law of effect.

**egg and spear technique**. A number-shape mnemonic system, representing each number with a distinctive shape.

**egocentric**. Self-focused. Characteristic of young children. As we grow, we learn to take the needs of others into consideration.

**eidetic memory**. Unusual ability to vividly remember images. Sequential images can be remembered as a composite, even though not presented together. Ability to view memories as if they were photographs.

**elaboration mnemonics**. Adding something to make it easier to remember. Includes storytelling and sentence formation. Every Good Boy Does Fine is an elaboration mnemonic for remembering the lines of a treble clef (EGBDF).

**elicited**. Classical conditioning assumes a response is elicited (dragged out) of the subject. The emphasis is on finding the right stimulus to trigger the desired response.

**Ellis, Albert** (1913-2007). Trained by one of Karen Horney's followers, believed we should battle the Tyranny of Should. According to Ellis, we make ourselves miserable by doing what others think we should do. If we worried less about that others thought, we'd be happier. For Ellis, thinking and happiness go together. How we think impacts how we feel. According to this view, thinking causes emotional consequences. Emotions don't stand by themselves. They are the result of your thinking; the product of your belief system.

In Ellis' terms, it's as easy as ABC. A is for Activating Event. Something happens: a sound in an adjacent room, perhaps. You think about that stimulus. And what you think

(Believe) determines your emotional Consequence. If you believe there is a burglar in the other room, you feel fear. If you believe there is a party you're not invited to, you feel envy. If you believe the sound was caused by visiting Aunt Betty, you're happy that you can now have the chat you've been wanting.

If emotional distress is caused by irrational thinking, the cure is to confront people with their irrational beliefs. Ellis is much more in-your-face than Rogers or traditional counseling. He doesn't avoid confrontation but seems to thrive on it. Although some clients may feel pushed by confrontation, they also seem to appreciate that therapy is moving along. You might be offended by what the therapist says but at least you know they are doing something.

Although described by others as a cognitive behavioral theory, REBT does not emphasize most of cognitive science: schemas, scripts, memory, learning, sensation, or information processing. His is a more informal cognition. He just means thinking. REBT is essentially a self-talk theory. What you say to yourself-your internal speech-is critical to your personal well-being.

Ellis would agree that people are constructivists, in a philosophical sense. We actively create our view of the world; constructing it out of our thoughts and ideas. We are creative problem solvers.

**emitted**. Operant conditioning assumes that subjects emit behaviors all the time. The consequence which follows a behavior determines the likelihood of the behavior occurring again.

**emotional distinctiveness**. The impact happy emotions have on memory. Generally, the addition of emotion and cognition.

**emotional disturbance**. For Ellis, we get emotionally upset because we care too much what others think. A learned pattern of behavior which can be changed.

**emotional intelligence**. Knowing what you feel and an awareness of what others are feeling.

**emotional memories**. A combination declarative memory and situational cues. Emotion aids the encoding of both semantic and episodic memory. Not a discrete category of memory.

**emotional self-regulation**. The ability to adjust your emotional response as a function of environmental changes.

**emotions facilitate behavior**. For Rogers, emotions are important. They help us decide which events and situations are important and which behaviors we should choose.

**empathy gap**. For Daniel Gilbert, a cognitive bias of not being able to predict how you will feel in the future.

**empiricism**. The belief that knowledge comes from experience. In science, the use of empirical methods (testing ideas by trying them out).

**empty gap**. The tip-of-the-tongue phenomenon. A common experience (~once a week).

**encoding specificity principle**. Training is best when the conditions of learning match the conditions of performance.

**encoding**. The first stage of three stages of memory, along with storage and retrieval. The input of information into memory.

**engagement**. One of Seligman's definitions of happiness. Flow.

**entorhinal cortex**. Medial portion of the temporal lobe. Connects the hippocampus to the cerebral cortex. Involved in semantic memory, spatial memory and navigation.

**environment**. Any context you are in.

**environmental cues**. The location, lighting and sounds are cues provided by the environment. They aid learning but are not easily controlled.

**environmental reinforcer**. The environment provides its own reinforcers: piles of leaves, puddles to splash, apples to eat. These reinforcers are not under your control.

**epinephrine**. A neurotransmitter which aids in the consolidation of memory.

**episodic buffer**. Part of Baddeley's model of working memory. Not to be confused with episodic memory. The episodic buffer is a short-term store for working memory.

**episodic memory**. Stories of your life, including what you did recently and as a child. A type of declarative memory.

**epistemic cognition**. The study of how knowledge is discovered.

**escape learning**. Physically leaving a space (house is on fire).

**eugenics**. Coined by Francis Galton. The belief that things should be done to improve the genetic quality of humans. Unfortunately, this often lead to the assumption that one group of people was more valuable than another, and that purity of race is better than genetic diversity.

**event marker**. In video editing, an indication of the beginning of a scene. In history, a plaque or statue used to commemorate an event. In learning, a record that a task has been done (drank six bottles of water).

**excessive punishment**. Bandura suggests three consequences of excessive punishment include compensation (superiority complex or delusions of grandeur), inactivity (apathy, boredom, depression) and escape (drugs, alcohol, television, fantasies, suicide).

**executive process**. Cognitive ability to switch tasks in response to new inputs and situational cues. Several prefrontal cortex regions are involved in this function.

**exercise**. Physical movement. In learning, practice (repetition) strengthens bonds and disuse weakens bonds; Thorndike's law of exercise.

**expanded retrieval strategy**. Also called expanded rehearsal strategy. Lengthen or shorten retrieval sessions based on the accessibility of memories.

**expectation schema**. In a general sense, all schema provide expectations. More specifically, socially developed rules about the future; rules (schema) about expectations. Expectations should not be too high (don't get your hopes up), should not be relied on (don't count your chickens before they hack) and should always be positive (the sun will come out tomorrow).

**expectation**. Rotter's term for estimating the likelihood of obtaining a reward. We like rewards but we really like rewards we know we can get. We'll turn down a bigger reward if a smaller reward is closer, faster or more of a sure thing. We do risk assessment and determine the likelihood of a receiving a reward. The reason we choose immediacy of rewards is they have a higher expectancy of coming true.

**experimental neurosis**. According to Pavlov, requiring too fine of distinction caused his dogs to bark and be unmanageable.

**experts**. High level of performance in a specific domain of knowledge or activity.

**explicit memory**. Information you can explicitly state. Also called declarative memory. Conscious recall. Includes semantic and episodic memories.

**external locus of control**. Rotter's term of the belief that our lives are determined by fate.

**external mnemonics**. Writing things down, getting them out of your head. Timers, diaries, journals, calendars, etc.

**externally-paced**. Instruction or activities which start when a signal is given (e.g., start of a race).

**external-paced events**. Time sensitive events that set the pace for you. Includes the light turning green, countering an attack, passing the ball before you get sacked, etc. Things that require immediate attention.

**extinction burst**. In operant conditioning, when extinction starts, behavior will increase before it decreases.

**extinction**. The reduction and elimination of a behavior as a natural consequence of removing its reinforcer.

**eye witness testimony**. Studied by Elizabeth Loftus. We are highly unreliable as witnesses.

# F

**face recognition** (face perception). Recognition and identification of a face. Processes in the fusiform gyrus of the temporal lobes. We are particularly good at identifying upright faces.

**facts**. According to Tangen, one of the three things that can be learned. Facts must be organized.

**fading**. Once a behavior is established, make the cue less obvious, eventually the dog should do it when you stop walking without your saying "sit."

**false memory**. Memories of things that didn't happen; can be induced by looking at modified photographs (Photoshop you in).

**far transfer**. Tasks with few or any identical elements. Learning A doesn't help you learn B.

**fast and frugal**. Decision making model of Gerd Gigerenzer. Use less information to make quicker and better decisions.

**fatigue method** (flooding). According to Guthrie, one way to break bonds of association is to present a stimulus so often that response is impossible.

**fear conditioning**. Classical conditioning of fear.

**feedback**. According to Thorndike, learning is best if practice with feedback (knowledge of effect).

**fictions**. Skinner's belief that free will is a superstition. People are responsible for their own behavior.

**fine motor skills**. Small muscles movements, develop after gross motor skills. Develop slower in boys and in girls (evens out by age 5 or 6). Includes, using a pencil, picking lint off carpet, and playing Lego.

**FITS**. An acrostic for Guthrie's Four ways to break habit: flooding, incompatible response, threshold and sidetracking.

**fixed interval** (FI). Reinforcer is given after the elapse of N minutes. Produces a scalloped pattern of behavior. After deadline is met, behavior drops off. Reinforcement given at set periods of time (e.g., every 3 minutes).

**fixed ratio** (FR). Reinforcer is given after every Nth response. Produces a steady rate of work. Paying per square of roof laid or piece of garment made. Reinforcement given as consequence of set number of responses (e.g., every 10th lever push).

**fixed theory of intelligence**. The traditional view of intelligence as being a fixed entity. In contrast to the incremental view of intelligence (that the more you learn the more intelligent you are). Your mindset (which view you take of intelligence) impacts your performance.

**flashcards**. Originally, a card with a small amount of information held up by a teacher as a learning aid for students. More commonly, a study aid created by students for themselves. A cue or prompt is written on one side of a card. The other side of the card contains the definition or response to the cue.

**flooded with memories**. The impact of classically conditioning and location cues. When you return to your childhood home or school, the rush of memories which are accessible to you.

**flooding method**. One of Guthrie's 4 ways to break a habit. Overwhelm (flood) with stimulation. Break a horse in by bronco riding. Applications are often unethical.

**flow**. Once of Seligman's definitions of happiness; a steady stream of meditation calm, usually from repeated action. In studying, an indication to switch to another topic.

**fluid intelligence**. Cattell's abstract thinking, in contrast to crystallized intelligence

**fluid movements**. Graceful and smooth continuous movements.

**focus**. What we select to mentally work on. Approximately the same as attention. Some disorders (e.g., ADHD) disrupt our ability to focus on a single course of thought or action. For most people, our attention span is about 15 minutes; longer for thing we interest us and less for things which don't interest us.

**focusing effect**. In perception, the brain makes one element stand out but it also makes all the other elements fade back. In decision making, the first feature or price presented is anchored and used to make all other relative judgements.

**forgetting curve**. Ebbinghaus' distribution showing recall for nonsense words drops off rapidly.

**forgetting**. Failure to recall previously learned information. Loss of declarative memories is thought to be the result of interference, while time is hypothesized as the loss of motor skills. First experimentally investigated by Ebbinghaus.

**formal operational stage**. Piaget's stage, abstract and symbolic thinking

**forward chaining**. Serial learning. Links are added to the end of the chain. The typical way of learning a song. A naïve mnemonic.

**forward conditioning**. The CS is presented before the UCS. Provides the quickest classical conditioning.

**four common problem-solving strategies**. Probably the most commonly used strategies are trial-and-error, root cause, hill climbing and means-end analysis.

**four consequences of punishment**. Punishment is broad, not good for changing specific behaviors. Punishment is temporary, only lasts if punisher is present. Punishment is vague, not clear what is being punished. Punishment stops all behavior, good and bad.

**frame**. A small bit of information in Skinner's programmed learning approach; in Gestalt theory, a point of view (frame of reference). A unit of learning in programmed instruction. Subject matter is broken down into small segments (frames) and arranged in a sequence. Each frame is a bit of information. In Gestalt theory, a point of view (frame of reference).

**framing effect**. A cognitive bias. We are influenced by the way things are stated (framed) in terms of loss or gain. "You could win a million dollars vs. you are highly likely to lose everything." "90% of patients have successful surgeries; 10% of patients die."

**framing**. The process of creating statements that represent a point of view (frame of reference). A cognitive therapy technique of clarifying thoughts.

**free recall**. Retrieval of items in any order you wish. Tend to recall last items best.

**free will**. The ability to make decisions without the influence of other people, circumstances or drugs. As drug usage increases, we have less and less free will.

**frequency**. Number of times in a set period of time. In vision, frequency encodes color. In audition, frequency encodes pitch. For generally, frequency is the number of times a stimulus is presented.

**frustration**. For Dollard and Miller, frustration and aggression is when one is unable to reduce a drive, such as when a goal is blocked. Anger for getting cut off in traffic is because our goal of getting somewhere quickly is blocked.

**frustration-aggression hypothesis**. For Dollard and Miller, getting cut off in traffic (frustration) leads to aggression (yelling).

**functional analysis**. Skinner. Looking at the behavior in a situation and identifying reinforcers. Not considering motive or intent.

**functional explanation**. As opposed to structural. Focus is on software. Behaviors is a result of learning, experience and environmental factors.

**functional fixedness**. Tendency to think objects only have one use.

**fundamental attribution error**. Also called the correspondence bias. Over-emphasize personality-based explanations. Under-emphasize situational influences

**fuzzy-headed thinking**. Tangen's term for diffused thinking.

# G

**Galton, Francis** (1822-1911). Galton believed that intelligence was a single faculty and that it was inheritable. He created many tasks to measure intelligence, and developed procedures for analyzing the data such as co-relation and percentile rank.

Galton applied the evolutionary views of his cousin (Charles Darwin) to the mind. In his book (Hereditary Genius, 1869), Galton attempted to show that greatness (in law, medicine, etc.) was a function of family heredity, not environment. It was survival of the intellectually fittest. Galton developed a number of tests to measure intellectual giftedness. For him, intelligence was measured by sensory capacities (allowing the best adaptation to the environment).

In his London laboratory, people paid to have their reflexes tested, their height (standing and sitting) measured, and their strength and reaction time recorded. To analyze his large collection of data, Galton developed methods of rank order, grouping by percentile rank, and co-relation (by looking at scatterplots).

**gambler's fallacy**. Also called the Monte Carlo fallacy. A type of mental averaging or limited time frame. Belief that random events currently more frequent than normal will in the short term future be less frequent than normal.

**game theory**. A method for studying logical decision making. Includes games of cooperation (winning requires players to help each other), zero-sum (if one player wins, another must lose) and symmetric games (a strategy is determined as a response to other strategies).

**Gardner, Howard**. Proposed a model of multiple intelligence which says we are born with specialized tendencies. Some people are prone to be better at processing certain types of information—musical, spatial, interpersonal, etc.

**gender schema theory**. Learning about gender from the surrounding culture, mental representation

**general intelligence**. According to Charles Spearman, intelligence is a general factor, probably biologically determined. General intelligence (represented by a capital G) includes everything we do and know. It is difficult to assess. It is easier to assess our performance on smaller tasks (represented by a lowercase g).

**Gigerenzer, Gerd**. Fast and frugal decision making.

**goal setting**. Identifying what you want and the intention of figuring out how to get it.

**goal state**. What the outcome will look like; where you want to be.

**goals**. Statements of outcome-oriented motivations. Food at the end of a maze.

**Google effect**. Less likely to remember information you believe is accessible online.

**gradient of approach**. Dollard & Miller's concept that the closer we get to something we like, the better it looks.

**gradient of avoidance**. Dollard & Miller's concept that the closer we get to something we dislike, the worse it looks.

**Grandma's law**. Eat your peas and you can have some dessert. Example of contingent rule.

**gross motor skills**. Large muscle movements, the first type to develop in children. Includes sitting, kicking a ball, maintaining balance and running.

**GROW**. A problem solving strategy developed in the UK. An acrostic of: goal, reality, options, way forward.

**Guthrie, Edwin R** (16-1959). Like Watson, Guthrie focused on observable behavior. Unlike Watson, Guthrie held that learning was a one-shot process of association. In contrast to classical conditioning, Guthrie's associationism followed Aristotle's concept of contiguity. Basically, Guthrie held that people tend to do what they did in a similar situation in the past. That is, the situation provides cues about how to behave.

Unlike Thorndike, Guthrie did not hypothesize a law of effect. It was simply a matter of contiguity. When a stimulus situation reoccurs, it tends to be followed by the same movement which followed it before.

 Guthrie's one shot learning did not preclude improvement. He maintained that practice doesn't improve performance because of repetition but because new S-R associations are being made. Although any single movement is learned in one trial, there is an infinite number of stimulus combinations possible. Each minute "movement" is learned one at a time but there are so many combinations to learn that one gets better at basketball.

A movement is a collection or pattern of motor responses. Movement produces stimuli (proprioceptive stimuli) in the muscles and tendons which help produce the next movement. An "act" is a collection of movements. Well-established movements and acts are called habits.

For Guthrie, each S-R connection is created at full strength and remains in full force until it is replaced by new learning. Habit strength is determined by the number of stimuli which can produce a response. To increase the strength of a habit (hanging up a coat), the proper cues must be associated with that response. According to Guthrie's theory, the best way to teach children to hang up their coats when coming in from play is not to make them do it after they forget. Instead, they should practice the whole sequence by going back outside, coming in, and hanging up their coats.

For Guthrie, the more stimuli which can be associated with a response the stronger the habit becomes. A director should not add more rehearsals to improve performance but more dress rehearsals.

There are four ways to break connections: sidetracking, fatigue, threshold, and incompatible response. In sidetracking, the person avoids the cues which produce the unwanted response (give up smoking while on vacation). The fatigue method presents a stimulus so often that response is impossible (ride a horse until it can't buck). The threshold method presents the stimulus in increasing increments (don't throw into the pool; get use to the water gradually). In the third method, an incompatible response is substituted (can't chew gum and smoke at the same time).

# H

**habit formation**. The process of acquiring a habit during repetition.

**habit loop**. A model of habit formation which assumes the presence of triggers and rewards. See the loop theory of habits.

**habit strength**. How strong a habit is. Includes how long you've had a habit, how much you want to change it, etc. Part of the theory of Hull.

**habit**. For Hull, the tendency to respond. For Guthrie, well established movements. For Watson, personality. For Dollard and Miller, earned associations between stimulus and response (S-R). They are temporary structures (habits can appear and disappear).

**half a biscuit for the same job**. An example of thinning. Providing less reward for the same task.

**half-second**. The optimal inter-stimulus interval (ISI) for forward classical conditioning.

**halo effect**. A form of confirmation bias combined with stimulus generalization.

**HAM**. Mnemonic for Guthrie's categories: habits, acts & movements.

**heuristics**. Mental rules. Fast and usually work but no guaranteed success.

**hierarchy of needs**. For Murray, needs exist at different levels of strength. Each need interacts with other needs. Need interactions and dynamics. For Maslow, deficit needs must be met before being (existential) needs. Physiological and safety needs must be met first, then belong and love. After these needs are met, people can work on their self-esteem and self-actualized needs.

**hierarchy of response**. For Dollard and Miller, we store our response options in a hierarchy where the most used are more readily available.

**higher criteria**. As a training aid, the bar is set higher. Baseball players practice with a heavier bat, runner race at higher elevations and students read the more difficult material first.

**high-level form of learning**. Learning that involves cognitive awareness and cortical processing. Examples include, learning lists of words, visualization and accommodation.

**highlighted foreground**. When perceiving an object, the mind emphasizes the object, making it stand out more from the background. At the same time, the background in deemphasized, making the distinction even more obvious.

**hill climbing**. Decision making technique that requires no planning. Move to next step closer to goal.

**hindsight bias**. I knew it all the time. Post hoc ego proctor hoc.

**hot cognition**. A term coined by Robert Abelson. A combination of logic and emotion. People change more easily moved to action if they are both inspired and reasoned with. In cold cognition, information is processed without emotion.

**how to learn lists**. Confirmed by Ebbinghaus, the best way to learn lists is repetition.

**Hull, Clark Leonard** (1884-1952). In his late teens, an outbreak of typhoid fever took the lives of several of Hull's classmates, and (according to Hull) damaged his memory. At the age of 24, Hull contracted polio, which precipitated his change from mining engineer to psychologist.

Hull was skilled at inventing equipment his needed to perform an experiment. For a study on the effect of tobacco on performance, he designed a system for delivering heated air (tobacco and tobacco filled) to the subjects so they would not know which experimental treatment they were receiving. Similarly, Hull constructed a machine to calculate inter-item correlations for a series of studies he performed on aptitude testing.

Not surprisingly, Hull believed that people are basically machines. His complex theory of learning is a combination of Newton's deductive method, Pavlov's classical conditioning, and Euclidean geometry.

For Hull, experimental observations were validity checks on the internal postulates he had previously deduced. Hull's Hypothetico-Deductive Theory includes habit strength (the tendency to respond), evenly spaced trials, and reinforcement. Using inferred state and intervening variables, Hull described learning as an interactive system of probabilities. Too complex for many and too theoretical for others,

Hull was a pioneer in using animal research to generalize to human behavior. Despite his poor eyesight and poor health, Hull set a standard of experimental excellent and theoretical integrity which still serves as a model today.

**human reflexology**. Bechterev description of psychology; behavior is completely explainable within a S-R (stimulus-response) format.

**hypothesis testing**. Scientific method; try to prove or disprove one possible explanation of why event occurred.

**Hypothetico-Deductive Theory**. Hull's complex theory of learning, habit strength and intervening variables. Piaget's stage, think like a scientist, generate a general theory

**iconic memory**. Memory buffer for visual images, lasts about ½ second.

**ideas**. Although people think, there is little agreement on how or why they do so. Although some thoughts, ideas and concepts may be innate, most are thought to be the result of mental activity.

**identical elements**. The best predictor of transferring what you've learned in one area to a new area. The more identical elements in common, the easier the transfer.

**idiographic**. Individual differences. Study of facts, not general principles.

**IKEA effect**. Dan Ariely's observation that people tend to place greater value on things they make or assemble. A type of effort justification.

**ill-defined problems** (ill-structured). Problems with unclear options. What gift to buy for someone's birthday.

**illumination**. An insight or ah-ha phenomenon. One of four stage of creativity: preparation, incubation, illumination and verification.

**imageless thought**. Historically, thoughts were considered to be miniature images of external objects. That is, thoughts were reducible to sensory images. But formal cognitive operations are not reducible to images; they are mental constructs or imageless thoughts.

**images**. Ancient philosophers believed people thought in images.

**imitation**. The second level of observational learning. Requires more intentionality than mirroring but less than modeling.

**immediate gain**. A common mistake is to focus on immediate or short-term gain, instead of trying to achieve long-term gain.

**implicit memory**. Knowing that's not perceived as memory. Includes procedural memory (how ride bike) & illusion-of-truth effect (don't remember source but think it's true because you've heard it).

**implosive desensitization**. Sudden confrontation of phobic situation (ethical?).

**impressions**. Ancient theory of memory. Just as pressure can leave a visible mark on objects (e.g., pencil on paper, chisel on stone), mental experience leaves an impression. Similar to memory but suggesting an emotional imprint.

**imprinting**. Some animals follow the first moving object they see, usually it is Mom.

**inattentional blindness**. Part of our perceptual filtering. We don't notice obvious things when engaged in another task (e.g., gorilla in the middle of basketball players).

**incentive**. Anticipated reward.

**incidental encoding**. Learning without trying.

**incompatible behavior**. Training an animal to sit on a mat instead of jumping on guests. Also called incompatible response.

**incompatible response method**. Can't do two things at once. Can't smoke and chew gum at the same time. One of Guthrie's four ways of breaking habits (FITS: flooding, incompatible response, threshold, sidetracking).

**incremental theory of intelligence**. In contrast to a fixed or entity view of intelligence. The view that the more you learn the more intelligent you are. Your mindset (which view you take of intelligence) impacts your performance.

**incubation**. Rest with the goal of solving a problem. Allowing the brain to work in the background. One of four stage of creativity: preparation, incubation, illumination and verification.

**infantile amnesia**. Inability to remember anything before age two or three. Cognitive structures haven't matured enough to store information.

**infographic**. A combination of information and graphic. A graphic summary of the steps of a process or the main points covered in a lesson. Isotypes and international symbols are examples of simple infographics.

**instinctive drift**. Tendency for wild animals to return to instinctive behaviors: tigers eat you, pot-bellied pigs root in living room.

**instincts**. Unlearned, innate patterns of response.

**instrumental conditioning**. Also called operant conditioning. Skinner's theory on reinforcement and punishment. Assumes future behavior is based on consequences of prior acts.

**intelligence quotient** (IQ). Score on a test, widely used predictor of school success. Tends to be stable over time.

**intelligence test**. Originally developed to predict school success. Not a measure of actual ability but of functional use of culture and language. Typically, an a-theoretical series of tasks designed to differentiate between people. Most modern intelligence tests load heavily on vocabulary.

**intelligence.** Although intelligence is conceptualized as the ability to acquire and use knowledge, it is most often operationally defined in terms of test scores.

Galton described it as a single entity, inherited biologically, and measured by reaction time tests. For Binet, intelligence was a cluster of abilities influenced by environment.

The intelligence ratio (coined by Lewis Terman) or intelligence quotient was originally proposed as the ratio of mental age to chronological age. Subsequently, the intelligence quotient (IQ, also coined by Terman) has been derived by comparing individual performance to group norms. Debate still rages on the nature of intelligence (general ability or a cluster of specialized faculties), and the relative importance of heredity and environment.

Thorndike proposed three types of intelligence: abstract, social, and mechanical. For Thorndike, Abstract intelligence (also called abstract reasoning) is the ability to manipulate words and concepts.

For Piaget, abstract thinking is the ability to discuss hypothetical situations and the systematic solution of problems.

**intensity**. Borrowed from physics, intensity is the amount of a force (electricity, heat, sound).

**intent**. Skinner maintains that the intent of a person doesn't count. It's whether their behavior is rewarding or punishing to the receiver.

**intentional behavior** (goal-directed). Includes talking, reaching, touching, solving simple problems.

**interactional synchrony**. Describes how a caregiver & baby respond to each other's emotional cues

**interactive images**. The key to remembering images is to make them interactive. In technical mnemonics, users of peg systems are often told to visualize weird images. This works only because interactive images are often weird.

**interference theory**. Theory of forgetting. Suggests that the more in-between events that have occurred, the less you will remember.

**interleafed practice**. Also called mixed or variable practice. Instead of learning task A before moving on to task B, interleafed practice spends some time on each task. Interleafed practice is good for long-term learning.

**intermittent schedules**. Any schedule of reinforcement that is not continuous. Intermittently rewarded behaviors tend to persist. Reinforcer is not obtained for every response

**internal locus of control**. Rotter's observation that believe they can control their lives. In contrast to external locus of control.

**internally consistent**. One of Tangen's CUSSIT criteria for testing a theory. A theory which is internally consistent is better than a theory which is inconsistent.

**inter-stimulus interval** (ISI). The amount of time between the CS and the UCS. Optimal is ½ second using forward conditioning.

**interval schedules**. Time-based schedules of reinforcement. In fixed interval, a certain amount of time passes before another reward will occur. This produces scalloped frequency rates. You work hard before a deadline but not until the next deadline approaches. In variable interval, an uncertain amount of time passes before another reward will occur. Produces a more steady rate of performance.

**intervening events**. The best predictor of forgetting is the number of events which have intervened between the original event and when you want to retrieve it. If no football games have intervened between the "great game" in high school, the glory of that day will be vividly remembered. If many other have occurred since high school, it will be a more distant memory.

**introspection**. In theology and philosophy, the term is used a self-contemplation. As used by early experimental psychologists, introspection was the observation (usually by trained individuals) on the internal processes and structures impacted by the presentation of a perceptual stimulus.

**involuntary attention.** One of Titchener's three types of attention. This type of attention occurs in response to a sudden noise or startle. The unplanned concentration of mental focus; usually the result of a sudden stimulus presentation (e.g., loud noise).

**irradiation**. For Pavlov, the spread of effect to other parts of the brain; stimulus generalization. (a spread of effect to other parts of the brain)

**irrational beliefs**. Beliefs about ourselves we learn from others and teach ourselves. Based on fears, insecurities and overestimating the importance of what other people think.

**irreversibility**. In Piaget's preoperational stage, children don't know objects taken apart and be put together again. They are at the Humpty Dumpty stage.

**isomorphism**. Similarity of forms or structures; for Wertheimer, apparent motion occurs in the brain but appears to be external.

**item familiarity**. Items in a list which are familiar to us are easier to remember.

**item similarity**. Items in a list which are similar to each other are easier to remember.

# J

**jackpot**. Great bursts of work deserve a greater than usual amount of reward.

**Jacobs, Joseph**. English school master who developed the digit span test as a way of assessing his students intelligence. People vary greatly in their ability to repeat digits, and can improve their performance with practice.

**James, William** (1842-1910). As a philosopher, psychologist and writer, James helped shift the focus from the search for mental structures and elements to the experimental study of mental functions. His concepts of self, stream of consciousness, pragmatism, and emotion are still cited today.

Best known for his philosophy of pragmatism, James helped redirect psychology into greater concern with higher mental functioning. A predecessor of functionalism, James was less concerned with the mental structures of the mind than with the functions it performs. His book (Principles of Psychology, 10) had a tremendous impact of the philosophy and direction of psychology. James shorter version of Principles, popularly known as "Jimmy," was a great commercial success. Chronologically between Wundt and Titchener, James was more of a mind-body dualist (Wundt was a parallelist, and Titchener a physical monist).

Influenced by Darwin, James maintained that behavior is adaptable, and that in order to survive psychologically people must be conscious of and adjust to their psychological and emotional environment. For James, consciousness is not a static picture but more like a flow of a river or stream. It is personal, ever changing, and has no breaks or cracks in it. James also held that consciousness is selective (we don't attend to everything) and that it is object oriented (does not deal with itself).

Although not a systematic theory, James envisioned a personal self. Although James discussed habit, instinct, memory, and reason, his theory of emotion has endured the longest. Before James, emotion was described as being the cause of action (I see the bear, I feel fear, I run). James maintained that emotion was a result of action (I see the bear, I run, I feel fear). Formally known as the James-Lange theory of emotion (after Danish physiologist C.G. Lange), it represented a major shift in thinking about emotion. Believed it takes 21 days to make a new habit, although it depends on the person.

**Jones, Mary Cover** (1897-1987). Pioneer of behavior therapy and systematic desensitization. First to show counterconditioning. Boy became less afraid, and then unafraid, of a rabbit if he could eat his favorite food at the same time.

**journey method**. Another name of the method of loci. You "journey" your way from place to place, remembering one item at each stop.

# K

**Kahneman, Daniel**. Israeli-American psychologist, Nobel laureate, and father of behavioral economics. Best known for his work in judgement and decision-making.

**keep-going signal** (KGS). A signal that indicates a behavior needs to continue in order to be rewarded. Similar to a personal trainer saying "Great; keep going."

**Kelly, George** (1905-1967). Personal construct theory. We build our personal view of the world through experiences. We use this structure of constructs (ideas, beliefs) to anticipate events. It allows us to react quickly to new information. We are logical but naïve scientists. We don't always revise our system and can end up with a distorted view of life.

Kelly was a predecessor to cognitive behavioral theories. We aren't restricted by drives or limited in response to stimuli. We are creative entities. For Kelly, you had a background in theater, if you want to change your personality, pretend for a while that you are different. Take on a role. Try it out. Dress and act like the person you want to be.

**knowledge**. The combination of facts and concepts.

L

**labels**. For Dollard & Miller, self-talk which allows unconscious conflicts to become conscious. Also called the Rumpelstiltskin effect.

**Lake Woebegone effect**. Tendency to overestimate achievements (based on Garrison Keillor fictional town where all the children above average). People estimate their intelligence, driving ability, popularity and problem solving skills as being above average.

**language acquisition device**. Theory that language is result of built-in mechanism. Explains why children learn language so fast from so few examples.

**language development**. The first sounds (1$^{st}$ month) are burps, grunts and sneezes) help exercise the vocal cords and create a dialogue with caregivers. By month two, infants coo and laugh out loud. They are learning the melody of speech. By month 3-4, infants practice consonants and follow the gaze of others. This is the start of joint attention. By six months, babbling starts and sounds not found in the primary language are pruned (discarded). This is when deaf infants fall behind in producing well-formed syllables. By nine months, babies have an accent when babbling. By 12 months, single word sentences (holophrases) are used and conversation turn-taking is common. From 18-24 months, there is a large spurt in vocabulary acquisition. By 24 months old, children have a useful vocabulary of about 200 words. By 6 years old, children use 4000 words and understand 800 words.

**late selection**. In perception, one of several filter theories. Late selection occurs when a stimulus is selected late in the processing chain. In contrast, early selection occurs when a stimulus is selected early in the processing chain.

**latency**. The amount of time between a stimulus and a response.

**latent inhibition**. Difficult to classically condition to CS that are familiar. Unusual stimuli work best.

**latent learning**. Bandura's position that learning can occur without being demonstrated. Reinforcement impacts demonstration but not learning.

**lateral thinking**. In decision making, trying a different tack; hit it from the side

**law of effect**. Thorndike view that behavior is controlled by its consequences. Behavior is controlled by its consequences

**law of exercise**. Thorndike's view that the more you do it, the stronger the bonds.

**law of readiness**. Thorndike's view that you must be developmentally and consciously ready to learn.

**laws of association**. Well established relationships or rules whose truth are beyond doubt (e.g., gravity, entropy, etc.). Aristotle proposed three laws of suggestion: contiguity, similarity, and contrast. Hume proposed 3 laws of association: contiguity, resemblance, and causality.

Thorndike proposed three laws of learning: readiness, exercise and effect. The Law of Readiness says subject must be able to perform task (e.g. cat must be hungry). According to the Law of Exercise practice strengthens bonds. Disuse weakens them. The Law of Effect maintains that the consequences of a behavior strength (or weaken) the S-R bonds.

**laws**. Well established relationships or rules whose truth are beyond doubt (e.g., gravity, entropy, etc.). Aristotle proposed three laws of suggestion: contiguity, similarity, and contrast. Hume proposed 3 laws of association: contiguity, resemblance, and causality. Thorndike proposed three laws of learning: readiness, exercise and effect. The Law of Readiness says subject must be able to perform task (e.g. cat must be hungry). According to the Law of Exercise practice strengthens bonds, Disuse weakens them. The Law of Effect says consequences of a behavior strength (or weaken) the S-R bonds.

**learned helplessness**. Learning that your actions have no impact on a situation generalizes to not trying when in other situations.

**learned optimism**. Learning that your actions can have impact.

**learning by doing**. John Dewey's educational theory that school should teach the math, reading and other information needed to do useful tasks (building, cooking and sewing). Learning should be practical (not theoretical), active (not passive), based in real life (hands-on) and guided (not dictated)

**learning process**. For Dollard and Miller, there are four units (steps) to learning: drive, cue, response and reinforcement.

**learning**. A semi-permanent change in behavior, knowledge and mental constructs.

**level of initial learning**. How well you learn something. It's initial level does not determine the rate of forgetting, only how long forgetting takes.

**lexical retrieval**. Searching for a desired word in your semantic memory.

**link & story systems**. Technical mnemonic techniques. Links are created by putting the words you want to remember into a chain or flow chart. Story mnemonics put the words or tasks you want to remember into a story (the car needs new brakes but want to stop by the bakery first).

**list length**. Confirmed by Ebbinghaus, the longer a list, the more difficult it is to learn. A natural outgrowth of this principle is to divide long lists into small lists.

**Little Albert**. In their 1920 article, Watson & Raynor show that fear can be classically conditioned. Their subject was a small child, named Albert B (affectionately called Little Albert). Watson classically conditioned the child to fear animal (stuffed and real).

**little g**. According to Spearman, a portion of general intelligence. Any task can be used as a sample of big G. This sample (a measure of little g) can be extrapolated as a measure of general intelligence.

**live fire**. A training exercise where real bullets are used. The idea is to give students a realistic sense of what an actual experience will be.

**LMNOP**. When children learn the alphabet, they learn these letters as a single word or chunk.

**lobes**. Cerebrum is divided into four anatomical regions (lobes). Cerebellum is divided into ten anatomical regions (lobules).

**local high**. When using the hill climbing decision making method, reach a point (not the top of the hill) where every choice is going down. Must go down to continue going up.

**location cues**. When we form a memory, we also record meta data. We extract the meaning of a situation, file away the elements needed to recreate the memory, and encode where we are and who we are with. These location cues help you remember in the kitchen but forget in the living room, and then remember again when in the kitchen.

**Locke, John** (1632-1704). Educated at Oxford, Locke is best known for his Essay Concerning Human Understanding, which was 17 years in the making. Locke disputed Descartes' emphasis on innate ideas. It was commonly held in Locke's time that morality was instilled in people by God. That is, people are born with knowing right from wrong.

In contrast, Locke proposed that the mind is as a blank slate (tabula rasa) and that ideas come from experience. Borrowing from his teacher Robert Boyle, Locke differentiated between primary and secondary qualities. Qualities are idea producers.

Primary qualities are inseparable from the object, and generate in us ideas of solidity, shape, and movement. Secondary qualities (such as color and taste) do not correspond to the physical world but are psychological in nature.

Locke was a dualist (mind and body exist separately), an empiricist (emphasized experience, and an associationist. He held that if the blind could be made to see, they would not be able to visually identify a cube because they had only experienced it by touch. They would need to learn to associate the shape with touch.

**locus of control**. Rotter's concept of a generalized expectation of behavior to get a reward. It is a univariant dimension that varies from internal to external. It reveals a person's view of contingent relationship between action and outcome. High internal locus of control believe rewards come primarily from action. High external locus of control believes reward come by chance.

**Loftus, Elizabeth**. Best known for her work on eye-witness testimony.

**longitudinal research** design. In contrast to cross-sectional research design. Studying the same people over time.

**long-term memory** (LTM). In contrast to short-term or working memory. Recall of facts and events not currently experiencing. Limit is difficult to measure but is quite large.

**loop theory of habits**. The theory that habits have a trigger, routine and reward, which then impacts another trigger.

**loss aversion**. Strong preference to avoid loss; twice as strong as desire for gain (Tversky & Kahneman).

**low-level form of learning**. Learning that requires very little cognitive awareness or effort. Examples include, resetting your internal clock, feedback loops and implicit memory.

# M

**magical thinking**. Believing that things will happen if you want it enough. Characteristic of Piaget's preoperational stage of development.

**masking**. Experimental procedure to test perception of visual or auditory stimuli. One stimulus is followed by interfering stimulus. Which is perceived depends on several factors.

**Maslow, Abraham** (1908-1970). Best known for his optimistic view of human nature and his hierarchy of needs. According to Maslow, self-actualization is a process, not an all-or-none phenomena. This process develops through five levels: physiological, safety, love & belonging, esteem, and self-actualization. Arranged in a hierarchy, development cannot proceed to the next level until those needs are met. Self-esteem, for example, can't be increased until one's physiological and safety needs have been met.

Maslow believed that people are inherently good and that the process to self-actualization is inevitable (if society nurtures it). People have a built in capacity for love which is shaped by society. Although each person is a unique individual, it is possible to distinguish between D and B motives. D motives are the result of deficiencies which must be met. In contrast, B motives are the result of growth needs, and seek to fulfill one's inner potential.

**Maslow's hammer**. Maslow's statement that if you have a hammer, all problems look like nails.

**massed practice** (normal practice). Long sessions of doing the same task. Good for short term gain.

**maximum certainly**. Being able to reliably do a task repeatedly. A criterion for measuring skills.

**maximum fluency**. Being able to speak or do a task smoothly. A criterion for measuring skills.

**meaning extraction**. We don't remember what we see or hear. We remember the meaning. We look at a scene but store only its meaning. We don't remember each flower in a field, we store "pretty."

**meaningful**. In general, we remember things that are meaningful to us. Chunking is a naïve mnemonic technique which creates meaningful units of information. Self-association with our experiences make some information easier to remember (e.g., your birth year in a series of numbers).

**means-end analysis**. Separation of goals and means. A decision making method. Progress is repeatedly measured and objectives adjusted in order to reach the desired end.

**mechanical intelligence**. The ability to use tools and machines.

**memory characteristics**. General aspects of memory, including that they are changeable, vivid, fragmented and fleeting.

**memory palace**. A technical mnemonic stategory for placing images in loctions. The palace can be a remembered real place or an imagined one. Sherlock Holms' use of the method of loci. Each room in the palace has objects, and each object is associated with a piece of information.

**memory systems**. Memory is composed of many systems, including declarative (semantic, episodic), implicit and working memory.

**memory**. The input (encoding), storage and retrieval (recall) of facts and concepts.

**mental inactivity**. Sleeping, relaxing or doing nothing about a learning session helps memory consolidation (Ebbinghaus, 15).

**mental rehearsal**. Thinking your way through a task or activity. Mentally practicing a speech or basketball shot. Not as good as real practice but better than none.

**mental representation**. We store things in our heads as abstractions (representations). We don't store actual scenes, we store a map.

**mental retardation**. The legal term for limited intelligence. A misnomer in that it assumes people with brain damage will eventually catch up (slow, retarded, needs more time).

**mental set**. A term introduced by Karl Marbe. When prior experience affects subject's current judgments, they are said to be responding with a mental set. Having generated a rule to solve prior problems, they continue to use the rule on current problems.

**mental strategies**. Cognitive plans for how to achieve a goal or perform a task. They form a hierarchy of practiced approaches.

**mental structures**. Another way of explaining thoughts. The basic processes used to process information, collections of rules or patterns of thought. There are three general types: schema, scripts and constructs.

**mental tests**. The term was coined by James McKeen Cattell to describe the perceptual and mental measurements he and Galton used.

**metacognition**. Thinking about thinking. Combines meta (larger than) & cognition (thinking); knowing what you know. The knowledge we have of what we know and can do. It included information used to monitor our progress.

**metaphors**. A tool for reasoning by simplification and comparison. Metaphors, analogies and similes have overlapping definitions. Metaphors are more general, analogies more practice, and similes more literary. Shakespeare's "all the world is a stage" is a metaphor. It is a general comparison. "This problem is like the one we dealt with last year" is a simile. "My cat is more affectionate than you" is an analogy.

**method of focal objects**. Identifying what problem characteristics have in common.

**method of loci**. A technical mnemonic strategy used by ancients Greeks and Romans. Combines images and places. Places (loci) are used as anchors or pegs. At each place, you store an image of what you want to remember. Information must be converted into images. Playing cards would be converted into images of famous people or people you know.

**methylphenidate**. A stimulant used to treat ADHD. Better known as Ritalin.

**Miller, George**. Best known for his work on chunking and his article "The magical number seven, plus or minus two." Proposed that working memory is composed of seven items or seven chunks, plus or minus two.

**mind as a computer analogy**. The basic approach of information processing. Perceptual systems are thought of as inputs, thinking as processes, and behaviors as outputs.

**mind map**. A version of a concept map. A single work is written in the middle of a page and other words, thoughts, pictures and information is linked to it. A visual guide to understanding a field of knowledge.

**mindfulness**. A process of attention focus. The emphasis is on the present moment, not thinking about the past or present. Common in Christian prayers and Buddhist traditions, the practice of mindfulness isn't limited to one religion or philosophy.

**minimum energy**. A task done with the least effort. A criterion for evaluating skills.

**minimum time**. A task done in the quickest time. A criterion for evaluating skills.

**mirroring**. The first stage of observational learning, seen within days of birth. Tilting your head to one side will be mirrored by the infant.

**misery-stupidity syndrome**. Tangen's parody of Dollard & Miller's term "stupidity misery syndrome." In Dollard & Miller's version, when we are unaware of a conflict (it is unlabeled) we are "stupid" about its existence, make poor decisions, and cause misery. In Tangen's version, we are miserable so we make stupid decisions. The more miserable we are, the less logical our thought process, and the more stupid we act.

**misinformation effect**. Episodic memory becomes less reliable when new but false information is introduced.

**mixed movements**. A combination of continuous and discrete movements.

**mixed practice** (varied or interleaved). Learning part of A, part of B and part of C, then returning to learn more of each.

**mixed skills**. A combination of discrete and continuous movements. Includes clicking a photo of a moving object, shooting space aliens as you fly your ship in a video game, and CPR (chest compressions are discrete and artificial ventilation is continuous).

**mnemonics**. Techniques for remembering better. Classified as naïve (done naturally) or technical (taught).

**modeling therapy**. Bandura's therapy using observation (modeling). Watch someone overcoming their fear of handling a snake, lose fear of snake. As client watches through a window, an actor models self-soothing behaviors while successfully approaching the snake. Client is invited to try it; some do it on first viewing. Film of productive behaviors works nearly as well as live viewing.

**modeling**. Bandura says it requires attention, retention and reproduction (converting mental image to behavior) and motivation (reason for doing it). Required a higher level of intentionality than mirroring or imitation.

**models**. Models are theories or parts of theories which have been converted into measurable

**morphological analysis**. Studying the whole system, including inputs, interactions and outputs.

**motivation**. For Bandura, includes past reinforcement (rewards), promised reinforcement (incentive) and vicarious reinforcement (expectation from seeing others rewarded.

**motives**. For Bandura, motives don't cause learning. They cause us to demonstrate what we have learned. For Murray, combination on underlying needs (latent needs) and external press. Motives influence which behaviors are expressed.

**movement produced stimuli** (MPS). For Guthrie, each tiny movement produces proprioceptive stimuli.

**movement**. Generally, types of behaviors (continuous, discrete, mixed). For Guthrie, small micro adjustments of muscles that form a chain.

**multiple contexts**. Learning tends to occur in a specific context. A method to counter reliance on context cues is to train or study in multiple contexts. Study at the kitchen table, the living room, the library, noisy places, quiet places, etc.

**multiple memory systems**. Memory is not a single entity. We have multiple systems. When one goes out the others, typically, still function.

**muscle memory**. Not stored in the muscles. Implicit memory.

# N

**naieve mnemonics**. Memory techniques people do automatically, without training. These include repretition, singing-rhymer, chunking and forward chaining.

**name recognition**. A memory task where you are shown a list and asked to identify those who were former classmates of yours.

**naturalistic observation**. Watching people in their native context.

**near transfer**. Practice of one tasks helps you learn a similar (near) task. Nearness is based on the number of identical elements.

**negate**. To take away.

**negative punishment**. For Skinner, stops behavior (punishment) by removing something, for example, taking away a teen's keys for being late. Punishing by removing something good (take away car keys).

**negative recognition**. Immediate knowledge that you don't know something. Don't have to search for the meaning of the word Ksuqoopf; immediately know you've never heard or seen it. Unclear how we know they without an exhaustive search.

**negative reinforcement**. For Skinner, there is an increase in behavior (reinforcement) caused by removing something, for example, taking away chores or canceling a loan. Rewarding by removing something bad (cancel debt).

**neglect of probability**. Tendency to disregard probability, particularly in uncertain situations. Small risks are completely neglected or greatly overrated.

**neural plasticity** (brain plasticity). Ability of the brain to change, shift activity and learn new things. Includes synaptic and non-synaptic plasticity.

**neurosis**. For Dollard & Miller, neurosis is a strong,

unconscious, unlabeled emotional conflict. The conflict means that people can't discriminate effectively.

**nicknames**. A naïve mnemonic technique. We tend to shorten people's names and titles to something easier to remember.

**no reward marker** (NRM). A signal that neither a reward or punishment has been earned. A "do it again" signal.

**Noh theater**. Japanese theater), practice separately, come together once: ichi-go ichi-e (one chance, one meeting).

**nonsense words**. Originally, a list of real words that had no connection to each other, so they were "nonsense." Later, Ebbinghaus used invented words, typically, consonant-vowel-consonant combinations.

**non-synaptic plasticity**. Ability of neurons to change.

**normal practice** (block practice). Learn A, then B, then C.

**normalcy bias**. Tend to under prepare for disasters because we underestimate its probability and its effect.

**note taking**. An external mnemonic technique. We write down what we want to study later. Most learning comes from reviewing and rewriting notes.

**number of decision options**. The more options we have, the less satisfied we are with our choice (one of the other ones was probably better).

**number-rhyme reversal system**. A technical mnemonic technique. Numerical pegs (1, 2, 3) are visualized as objects that rhyme (sun, shoe, tree). In order to remember numbers, compound images are formed (sun-tree-tree-shoe would be 1331).

**number-rhyme system**. A technical mnemonic; a type of peg system. The pegs are rhymes for numbers. Instead of 1-2-3, you use sun, shoe and tree. For each peg, you visualize an item. If you want to buy bread, milk and socks, you visualize the sun eating bread, milk in a shoe (or a cow in a shoe), and a tree of socks.

# O

**object classification**. Dividing objects into groups based on some characteristic. Mental sorting. If used in encoding, improves recall. Also improves performance if used in recall, regardless of whether used in encoding or not.

**object permanence**. For Piaget, learning that out of sight is not out of existence.

**object schemas**. Cognitive rules we carry about objects (it's okay to break them, every object should be horded, etc.).

**observational learning**. Most associated with Bandura. More than observing, it is encoding that improves retention. More effective if the model is admired or similar to observer, the behavior has a functional value and if the outcome goal is valued.

**one-shot learning**. Brain is thought to make simple connections. According to Guthrie, individual movements are learning on the first pairing; learning appears to be gradual because there are so many possible combinations of S-R pairings.

**open environment**. A problem space where no clear rules are guaranteed to work. An ill-defined problem. Unpredictable; the environment is always changing. Requires dynamic adjustments. Includes playing jazz, debating, boxing, and improv.

**operant conditioning** chamber. Skinner build an air conditioned, glass box crib for his daughter. At one point it was commercially available but it was not a popular success. Skinner called it a Baby Tender, critics called it a Skinner Box.

**operant conditioning**. Also called instrumental conditioning. The use of Skinner's principles of reinforcement and punishment.

**operant**. For Skinner, a class of behavior, not a single response. Rewards impact operants and affect all phone answering behavior (not just the one you want).

**operational definition**. Defining a variable by specifying things that can be done (operations). Clear definitions not open to interpretation; don't infer internal states. Hunger is not "appears hungry" but hours without eating. Intelligence can be operationally defined as a test score (IQ), running speed or behavior scored by a panel of judges. Operational definitions allow researchers to know what previous researches did and how they defined their variables.

**opposites**. One of Aristotle's laws of association. A clear contrast with a known object allows "one of these things is not like the other" comparisons.

**order of presentation**. Serial learning doesn't allow items to be rearranged into more meaningful units. If order of presentation is up to you, items can be arranged at will. Most important thing first takes advantage of primacy. Most important thing last takes advantage of recency.

**ordinal relationships**. Larger than or smaller than. Includes ratings, ranks and relative judgments. Think of it as lining up for school recess by height.

**outline**. A tree-like structure for organizing thoughts. Main points are followed by indented sub-points, which are followed by further indented sub-sub-points. A common way to take notes.

**overestimate transfer of learning**. A cognitive bias. We tend to overestimate the value of prior experience in solving current problems. The best predictor of transfer is the number of identical elements.

**overlearning**. People tend to stop studying too soon. Memory increases with repetitive trials. For Ebbinghaus, overlearning is continuing to study after a list has been learned error free.

**overt behaviors**. According to Watson, anything which can be seen or measured.

**pace**. The initiation of and duration of an instruction or activity. Slow walk vs. speed walking.

**panic attack**. Sudden but temporal experience of extreme fear and anxiety. Characterized by rapid breathing, heart rate, faint. Feels like heart attack. Peaks in about 10 minutes.

**panic disorder**. Repeated attacks of anxiety. More common in women and teens. Characterized by sweating, trembling, chest pain, palpitations and fear of dying.

**partial reinforcement**. As opposed to continuous reinforcement. Behavior that is partially reinforced tends to persist.

**part-set cuing**. Having seen a complete set and given a part of that set as a cue, remembering the whole set is more difficult than if no cue had been given.

**passive store**. In theory, a place where we store information with no further processing or degradation of it. Long-term memory is often described as a passive store.

**past punishment**. Not part of Skinner's theory but a cognitive factor which impacts performance. A part of expectation.

**path integration**. Darwin's explanation for birds being to find their way back to the nest using continuous integration of movement cues.

**Pavlov, Ivan Petrovich** (1849-1936). A Nobel prize winning physiologist, Pavlov is best remembered for his description of classical conditioning. A believer in the primacy of physiology, Pavlov thought psychology to be a fad. As far as he was concerned, psychological problems were physiologically based but currently unexplained.

Pavlov's classical description notes that the presence of an unconditioned stimulus (food) produces an unconditioned response (saliva of a given amount; varying somewhat between trials and between dogs). After sufficient pairings of the food with another, previously unused stimulus (e.g., light), the conditioned stimulus (light) could bring about a response (conditioned response). The conditioned response was weaker than the unconditioned response (i.e., less saliva) and forgettable (if repeated too often without food being presented).

Pavlov called the conditioned response "psychic secretion," and explained it as being the result of higher cortical involvement. For Pavlov, reinforcement was in terms of reiteration. One reinforced behavior as in reinforcing steel (added more of it). Pavlov believed that mental functioning was completely neurological. He proposed a "dynamic stereotype," a neurological mapping of the environment.

**PDCA**. A problem-solving strategy. Stands for plan, do, check and act (or adjust). Some versions add an O at the beginning for "observe."

**peg systems**. Technical mnemonics which are versatile but require time and effort to set up. Pegs are like kindergarten coat racks: one item per peg. The pegs can be reused. Includes number-rhyme, number-shape, alphabet rhyme, alphabet-concrete image systems.

**performance characteristics**. Criteria for evaluating skills, including maximum certainty, maximum fluency, minimum energy and minimum time.

**permastores**. Some things are more easily remembered than others, for no apparent reason. They just get stuck (frozen) in the mind. Coined by Harry P. Bahrick.

**perseverance**. Continuing on, not quitting. Thought to be a bigger factor in success than talent.

**perseveration**. The continued processing of an item after practice or rehearsal ends.

**person as scientist**. The belief people should act rationally. A contradiction to how people actually behave.

**person schemas**. Our knowledge of how people in general act.

**personal construct theory**. For Kelly, we construct our own world view from ideas (constructs).

**personal constructs**. Part of Kelly's cognitive theory. Our belief system is composed of ideas (constructs) which vary in importance and stability. Each person builds their own conceptual reality, which is changeable with some effort.

**personal experience**. Items in a list which relate to our personal experience are easier to remember. A sequence of random number which includes your year of birth will be easier to remember.

**personality**. For Rotter, it is a changeable collection of thoughts, environment and behavior interactions. In general, a theoretical construct to explain consistencies in human behavior.

**pessimistic style of thinking**. The tendency to believe that bad things will never change, they are your fault, and you can't do anything correctly.

**phonological loop**. Part of Baddeley's model of working memory. How what we read is converted into sounds and then meaning is extracted.

**photographic memory**. A myth of memory: the ability to remember everything you see. In reality, some people are very good at recalling pages of text in great detail (spatial memory) or to visualize images (eidetic memory) but no one can remember everything they see.

**photographs**. An excellent external mnemonic tool for remembering your childhood.

**physical monism**. The belief that nothing exists but matter. Concludes that there is nothing after death.

**Piaget, Jean** (1896-1980). Swiss psychologist best known for his stage theory of cognitive development. Born and raised in Neuchatel, Switzerland, Piaget was always interested in biology and zoology. After earning his Ph.D. in biology, he became interested in psychology, particularly in how cognition develops. While working for Binet at the Sorbonne, Piaget noticed that children don't solve problems like adults do. Children are not miniature adults but have their own distinctive style of thinking which develops in stages.

Piaget proposed four stages of cognitive development: sensorimotor, preoperational, concrete and abstract.
The sensorimotor stage occupies the first two years of a child's life. In this stage, children acquire motor control, and learn to interact with objects and accommodate to the world.

In the preoperational stage (ages 2 to 7), children acquire language. Their thinking is egocentric and contradict themselves but are not bothered by it. They can name objects, think intuitively, and argue their point of view. They cannot argue from someone else's point of view, and believe that tall and thin containers hold more than short, fat ones).

In the concrete operational stage (ages 7 to 12), children can manipulate numbers, develop rules for classifying objects, and acquire conservation (e.g., know that shape is not the same as quantity).

In the formal operational stage of development (ages 12 to adult), children acquire abstract thinking, can discuss hypothetical situations, and perform systematic searches for solutions.

**picture superiority effect**. Lists of images are easier to remember than lists of words. Originally proposed by Allan Paivio. assumes that pictures are easier to encode because they are more symbolic, and that concrete concepts have dual encoding (verbally and as image). Images generate a verbal label but words don't generate images. Results can be explained by familiarity and distinctiveness. Highly similar pictures are not easy to learn or remember.

Understanding words is fast; we are slow at understanding pictures. But once understand, icons are good if they are not similar. Images may be better organized when paired because they form an interactive composite image.

**pie chart models**. Helpful for showing the relative size of one segment versus the whole.

**pillory**. A device used for public humiliation and confinement (head and arms). Rocks and insults were thrown as prisoners (positive punishment). The immobility of the restraints and shunning were negative punishments.

**placebo effect**. Told that substance will help them, people report that it (sugar pill, saline injection, etc.) impacts them. Subjects report positive effects (reduced pain, etc.), negative effects (increased headaches, etc.) or both.

**plan for failure**. In case, Plan A fails, have a Plan B. If you fall off the wagon, have a contingency plan (who to call, where to go, etc.).

**plasticity**. Easily changed, adjusted or changed.

**pleasure**. The subjective experience of happiness.

**Pollyanna effect**. The tendency to remember pleasant words better than unpleasant.

**positive punishment**. Giving something following a behavior that makes it less likely for the behavior to continue (punishment). Positive punishment would include yelling, spanking, frowning, etc. The giving of something bad.

**positive recognition**. The end of search. Recognition that you have found what you were looking for. No immediate result is guaranteed.

**positive reinforcement**. Giving something following a behavior that make it more likely for the behavior to continue (reinforcement). Positive reinforcement would include candy, smiles, money (a raise at work), etc. The giving of something good.

**post-purchase rationalization**. Finding reasons for having made a decision.

**practical intelligence**. One of Sternberg's three kinds of intelligence (Triarchic Theory of Intelligence, along with creative and analytical. Practical intelligence is the ability to have street-smarts, handle daily living and reach goals.

**practical memory**. What you know from personal experience in the world (which trees lose leaves, how horses stand, etc.).

**practical problem solving**. Although our memory for names decreases over time, our ability to solve practical problems doesn't seem to diminish with age.

**practice effects**. Previous exposure to a test or task makes it easier.

**practice sessions**. Periods set aside to study or practice a skill.

**practice**. Repetition or what you do (practice law, practice medicine, etc.).

**praise and affection**. Excellent reinforcers with no side effects.

**predictably irrational**. Dan Ariely's term for how our cognitive structures and biases influence to make predictable but irrational (more emotional) choices.

**Premack principle**. In a free choice, activities higher on your hierarchy of preferred tasks can be used as reinforcers for items lower on the list. If you dislike taking out the garbage but really dislike answering your email, taking out the garbage can be used as a reward for processing email.

**preoperational intelligence**. Piaget's term for how children think before they acquire language.

**preoperational stage of development**. For Piaget, a period when children have no cognitive rules about conservation and do not use logical thinking. It is also when language is acquired (ages 2-7).

**preoperational thinking**. For Piaget, children have no logical thought processes and don't understand conservation (rocket fuel is the same whether it is in a large bucket or a small glass).

**preparation**. Problem formulation, study and skill acquisition. One of four stage of creativity: preparation, incubation, illumination and verification.

**prerequisites for good decision making**. Horney suggests four items: being aware of our real feelings, creating out own set of values, making a deliberate choice between 2 opposite possibilities and taking responsibility for the decision we make. She might also add that the emphasis should be on an individual's current situation rather than on the past.

**primacy**. The tendency to remember the first things on a list, assuming serial recall.

**primary distinctiveness**. Context impacts recall. The von Restroff effect (colored word in middle of list).

**primary drives**. Dollard and Miller. physiological processes. Strong, primitive needs of deficit. In contrast to secondary drives. Reduction of one type of drive doesn't reduce the other type.

**primary memory**. Short-term memory or working memory. The memory system you access first.

**primary reinforcer**. For Dollard and Miller, events that reduce primary drives (physiological processes. Based on physiological processes and deficits.

**priming**. A part of implicit memory. Exposure to one stimulus can impact a later stimulus. Occurs in many sense modalities; works best when cues and responses are of the same modality. Can be seen as a lexical decision tree. Teller is found faster (positive priming) if proceeded by "bank" than by "river." Negative priming is hypothesized but has little empirical support.

**proactive interference**. What you know impacts what you are learning. Existing schema influence present inputs. Calling your current love by your old love's name.

**problem definition**. The difference between where you are and where you want to be.

**problem finding**. Discovering that there is a problem, whether it is temporary or long-term, whether it is easily solvable, and who is most likely to solve it.

**problem shaping**. Trying different ways of looking at a problem. Pushing on a problem's conceptual shape to see if it can fit in a round hole. Revising a question until it is in a form you can answer.

**problem space**. The entire problem and all of its components. Includes problem definition, brainstorming, solution selection, hypothesis testing and implementation.

**problem state**. Either the current condition (state) of a problem (e.g. damage report) or a nickname for a problem statement (e.g. a brief overview of the problem needed to be solved).

**problem-solving opportunity**. A cognitive reframe of trouble.

**procedural memory**. Type of implicit memory. Knowing how to do procedures, tasks and actions. Doesn't include being able to explain how you do it.

**productive failure**. Learning from our mistakes. The concept popularized by Manu Kapur that struggling helps us learn.

**programmed instruction**. A method of instruction based on Skinner's behaviorism; small instructional steps, each followed by immediate feedback. An application of Skinner's operant conditioning to education. It uses a teaching machine (computer or books with small quizzes) to present small bits of information in ordered sequence, followed by immediate feedback. Each frame or bit of info must be learned before allowed to proceed to the next section. It assumes proceeding to the next section is rewarding.

**programmed learning**. Based on Skinner's approach to education. The lessons are self-paced, given in small bits, and provides immediate feedback.

**proportional reward**. More reward is given for more effort.

**propositional thought**. Piaget's stage of thinking which uses abstractions. Not mastered until adolescence.

**proprioceptive stimuli**. According to Guthrie, stimuli produced by muscle movement.

**prospective memory**. Remembering to do things in the future (go to the doctor, pick up laundry, etc.). Memory error of this type is often a concern of the elderly. Can be lack of record keeping (calendar) or lack of cues.

**proverbs**. A naïve mnemonic technique. Short phrases of folk wisdom. Includes, read in the morning, sailors take warning; spring forward, fall back; and dessert is sweeter than desert because it has more Ss.

**proximal zone of development**. Vygotsky's term for the difference between what you can learn on your own and with the help of others.

**proximity**. A Gestalt principle of grouping by closeness in time or space.

**psychic secretions**. Pavlov's term for a conditioned response.

**punishment marker**. A signal that a behavior was incorrect and that a punishment has been earned. The classic "wait until your father gets home" signal. Not recommended.

**punishment**. A consequence that makes a behavior less likely to reoccur as long as punisher is present. Positive punishment is giving something bad (yell, scowl). Negative punishment is taking away something good (car keys, computer time). Suppresses all behavior; strong unwanted side effects. Anything which tends to reduce the frequency of behavior.

**purposeful behaviorism**. According to Tolman, behavior is purposeful, goal directed, and molar (not reducible to instincts or reflexes).

**puzzle box**. Thorndike experiment where a hungry cat learned to pull a string in order to leave a box to get the food in a bowl placed just outside the box.

**pyramid models**. Helpful for showing the sequence and interdependence of stages or processes. Maslow's model of needs is a pyramid model.

# Q

**qualitative research**. Typically, surveys, interviews and focus groups. Good for choosing between options.

**quantitative research**. Experiments and studies that measure how much or how far things have changed.

# R

**RADAR**. An acronym of radio detection and ranging.

**rapid verbal, slow motor forgetting**. Tangen's summary of Ebbinghaus' forgetting curves for semantic material and motor skills.

**ratio schedule**. Frequency-based schedules of reinforcement. In fixed ratio, a certain number of responses must occur to receive another reward. You are paid per widget. In variable ratio, an uncertain number of responses must occur to receive a reward. This is the basis of gambling. Produces very high rates of performance that are very resistant to extinction.

**rational choice theory**. The idea that people make decisions by evaluating options logically.

**rational emotive behavioral therapy**. Ellis. It is primarily a cognitive behavioral therapy with 4 fundamental processes: perception, movement, thinking and emotion. Thoughts and emotions frequently overlap, so much of emotion is evaluative thinking.

**rational emotive therapy**. Ellis maintains people should confront their irrational beliefs and be persuaded to adopt rational ones. Ellis redid the theory, calling it rational emotive behavioral therapy.

**rational psychotherapy**. The first model by Ellis. The focus was on rational, not irrational, thinking. It was criticized for neglecting emotions. Ellis redid the theory, calling it rational emotive therapy.

**rationality**. The use of logic or reason when making decisions.

**RDO**. A typical acronym for regular day off.

**reasoning**. For Dollard and Miller, reason is an internal chain (or groups of chains) of drive, cue, response and reinforcement.

**recall**. The retrieval part of memory Recollection from a cue. Can be free recall (remember list items in any order) or serial recall (remember list backwards or forwards). The retrieval part of memory. Can be free recall (remember list items in any order) or serial recall (remember list backwards or forwards).

**recency**. The tendency in free recall to remember the most recent items.

**reciprocal altruism**. Mutual benefit behaviors; you scratch my back, I'll rub your feet.

**recognition errors**. Recall dimension (up-down) but not remember which particular action to do (up or down). Don't confuse dimensions (up-down, in-out, left-right).

**recognition**. Selecting from available choices; multiple choice items A memory retrieval task that involves choosing the correct item from an array. Sometimes easier than recall, sometimes more difficult.

**recollection**. Perception is the collect of sensations; memory is their re-collection.

**reconsolidation**. Process of changing long-term memories. Previously consolidated memories are recalled, paired with new but similar experiences, then reconsolidated. Mixed results. Evidence memories are not always permanent.

**reduction mnemonics**. Mnemonic techniques to reduce the amount of information to be recalled, such as acronyms and nicknames.

**reduction**. Changing a problem into one that can be more easily solved.

**reframing**. A cognitive therapy technique of rephrasing statements with a more positive or alternative interpretation. A way of disputing irrational thoughts.

**rehearsal**. Put everything together; repetition Naïve mnemonic of repeating a word or phrase to keep it in memory.

**reinforcement** (Dollard & Miller). Anything that increases the likelihood of particular response. They differentiate between primary reinforcers (reduce primary drives) and secondary reinforcers (reduce secondary drives).

**reinforcement** (education). The reiteration of information. Learning is like building a wall with reinforced concrete.

**reinforcement** (Skinner). Anything which occurs after a behavior which tends to increase the likelihood of its reoccurring. A consequence that makes a behavior more likely to reoccur. Positive reinforcement is giving something good (smile, candy). Negative reinforcement is taking away something bad (canceling debt, not have to do chores).

**reinforcement value**. Rotter's term for the size of a reward. We use the likelihood (E) and reward size (RV) to determine our behavior.

**reinstatement of context**. For Baddeley, visualizing a prior context allows a majority of the context-sensitive memory to be restored.

**reinstatement**. In classical conditioning, after a behavior has been extinguished, a presentation of the UCS brings the conditioning back.

**release from proactive interference**. Switching from one task when tried to another (but different task) increases performance.

**reminiscence**. Memory; to recollect the past.

**repetition**. Doing something over and over. Sometimes called rehearsal.

**representation of knowledge**. The hypothesis that information is stored in the brain in mental structures.

**repressed memory** (psychogenic amnesia). Doesn't exist.

**research**. In decision making, an attempt to find existing solutions to similar problems.

**resilience**. The ability to "bounce back" from stress and trauma.

**resistance to forgetting**. The idea that some things are harder to forget than others.

**response**. Behavior. One of four Dollard and Miller's four units of learning. A behavior or act.

**rest**. Incubation period to allow a problem to "perk."

**retention**. The amount of facts memorized. Ebbinghaus provided the first experimental description of a retention curve (the amount of recall over time).

**retrieval failure**. The hypothesis that things are stored in the brain (available) but can't be recalled (not accessible). Can't find the tags or handles need to retrieve a memory.

**retrieve often**. A study technique. Retrieving material from long-term memory is better than having another encoding trial. The more information is retrieved, the more accessible it is.

**retroactive interference**. The tendency for new inputs to influence existing schema. What you learn screws up what you previously knew.

**retrograde analysis**. Problem solving strategy to work backward to solve a problem. In chess, determining which moves led to a given position.

**review**. Going over previous events or knowledge. For studying, consolidating and rewriting notes makes a good review.

**reward marker**. A signal that the correct behavior was performed and reward has been earned. A clicker or whistle works well as a reward marker.

**reward size**. One of Rotter's factors in decision making.

**reward**. Something you like to receive or compensation for a job well done.

**rewrite your notes**. Based on the idea that restructuring material improves your memory of it. Related to but not the same as Craik & Lockhart's level of processing theory.

**rhinal cortices**. The regions surrounding the hippocampus, involved in learning helplessness.

**rhymes**. An effective naïve mnemonic. I before E…

**robust effect**. An outcome that holds true in many situations and with many types of information. Chunking, for example, works with words, numbers, pictures, etc. It is a robust effect.

**root-cause analysis**. A problem-solving strategy to look for basic causes, such as asking if the item is unplugged.

**rooting**. Pigs instinctively dig in the dirt with their noses.

**rote learning**. Memorization by repetition. Good for things you want quick access to.

**Rotter, Julian** (1916-2014). Best known for internal-external locus of control. Combined behaviorism plus cognition. What we know about the environment impacts what we do.

There are three component parts to Rotter's system. First, as Skinner would predict, we look at the size of the reward. We prefer big rewards over small rewards. In general, we want the biggest reward we can get.

Second, there is the expectancy of the reward. We like rewards but we really like rewards we know we can get. We'll turn down a bigger reward if a smaller reward is closer, faster or more of a sure thing. We do risk assessment and determine the likelihood of a receiving a reward.

Third, Rotter's main point is that we combine our calculations of expectancy (likelihood) and reinforcement value (reward size). This explains why people stay is safe low-paying jobs, and why people stay in predictable unhappy marriages. Rotter is suggesting that we are more rational than we realize. As our environment changes, we use rules to determine what to do.

Rotter expanded his concept of expectancy to a broader, more generalized expectation: locus on control. Our locus of control is our view of the contingency between what we do and what we get. If we have an internal locus of control, we tend to believe that what we do helps us get rewards. An "internal" tends to be more political, proactive, and optimistic. They assume they will be successful because expect their behavior to produce rewards. Consequently, internals try to gather more information, change their environment, and influence others. They are also more likely to be anxious. Since they believe what they do matters, they take responsibility for everything...whether it's their fault or not.

In contrast, "externals" tend to conform, and don't expect much of life. They believe life is a matter of chance, fate or luck. Externals tend not to take responsibility for anything. Since they believe that what they do doesn't impact what they get, there is little reason to work too hard at changing the inevitable. They are more susceptible to what Seligman called "learned helplessness."

**Rotter's formula**. The likelihood of a behavior occurring is a function of the likelihood of getting a reward and the size of the reward.

**rule of thumb**. A heuristic.

**Rumpelstiltskin effect**. Dollard & Miller's metaphor for the need to label. In the fairy tale the power of Rumpelstiltskin is neutralized when he name is revealed. When we can label our unconscious fears, they too lose their power.

# S

**saccade**. Fast movement of a body part. In vision, quick, simultaneous movement of eyes, vertically or horizontally. In contrast to birds, humans don't use steady stare; eyes always moving.

**same order every time**. Retrieval is best when encoding trials present items in the same order every time.

**satisficing**. A combination of satisfaction and sacrifcing.

**savings**. For Ebbinghaus, the number of time needed to relearn a list.

**scaffolding**. Also called instructional scaffolding. Bruner's concept that new learning must be built on old learning.

**scalloped**. The result of fixed interval rewards. The behavior will rapidly increase before a deadline than drop off dramatically.

**schedules of reinforcement**. Five schedule include continuous, fixed interval, fixed ratio, variable interval and variable ratio. For Skinner, patterns of response related to when reinforcement is given. Types include: continuous (reinforcement of every correct response), fixed interval (given for a correct response after a set period of time), fixed ratio (given for a correct response after a set number of correct responses), variable interval (given for a correct response after a varying period of time), and variable ratio (give for a correct response after a varying number of correct responses).

**schema characteristics**. Schema develop over time. They gradually build up. They are a product of our experience, unique to use and automatically triggered. Any sensory input can trigger a schema, individually or collectively. Schema are context sensitive.

**schema development**. We start with one category, adding to it or dividing it into new categories only when we need to. If we start with cat, we might then learn bad cat, good cat, cartoon cat, dead cat, lion, tiger, etc. The more knowledge we acquire, the more categories we have.

**schema hierarchy**. We access schema in order from most used to least used.

**schema limits**. Schema are automatically activated by stimulus features, so you can't stop them from occurring. Like other cognitive biases, the fewer the samples you have, the stronger the schema is. "All the people I know" is easier if you only know a few people. "Everyone is like this" is hard if you know people from a wide range of backgrounds and experiences.

**schema uses**. Schemas organize thinking, help plan behaviors and allow us to anticipate events ahead of time. They also allow us to fill in missing details.

**schema**. Cognitive rules we develop through culture and experience. Categories of thought, information and knowledge. Can be used as singular and plural; or schema for singular, schemata for plural). A mental representation developed from experience of what to expect. A mental model of how the world works, what people are like and what can be expected in various circumstances.

**scripts**. A type of schema. Composed of common social interactions you can predict. Hello, hello; How are you, fine how are you.

**secondary attention**. One of Titchener's three types of attention. This type of attention occurs as a matter of voluntary choice.

**secondary circular reactions**. Part of Piaget's sensorimotor stage (4-8 months). Infant does something on purpose to get a care giver's reaction. Repeating drops toy or bottle.

**secondary distinctiveness**. The first you do or see something.

**secondary drives**. For Dollard & Miller, learned drives that are associated with primary drives. In contrast to primary drives. Reduction of one type of drive doesn't reduce the other type.

**secondary reinforcer**. For Dollard & Miller, they are originally neutral but they acquire their reward value when associated with primary reinforcers. events that reduce learned drives (acquired drives)

**self-control therapy**. Bandura's theory includes three parts: behavioral charts (track behavior), environmental planning (change the environment, remove or avoid cues) and self-contracts (written, witnessed, specify contingencies specified).

**self-discipline**. Roughly the same as self-control.

**self-efficacy**. For Bandura, self-knowledge of personal ability (competence).

**self-paced events** (self-paced instruction). Some time constraints but when you start is up to you. Begin your speech when you want, start your long jump at will, etc. Perform when you want.

**self-punishment**. Self-administered reproof or blame. The opposite of self-reinforcement.

**self-regulation**. Bandura's version of self-concept or self-esteem. Includes three steps: self-observation (tracking behavior), judgment (compare to a standard) and self-response (reward compliance, punish failure).

**self-reinforcement**. Self-administered rewards or praise. The opposite of self-punishment. The rewards one gives to one's self; internal motivation.

**self-schemas**. What you know about yourself.

**self-stimulation** of the brain. Rats implanted with electrodes in the lateral posterior hypothalamus push level compulsively. In humans, can be used as operant reinforcer.

**self-sustaining schema**. Schemas are self-sustaining. Once we have a prejudice or stereotype, we don't have to do anything for it to continue. Schema continue until we have enough examples of other people who don't fit our predetermined mold.

**self-talk**. For Ellis, our internalized sentences determine our thoughts and emotions.

**semantic encoding**. Encoding on the basic of what words or events mean, in contrast to encoding on the basis of how things sound or look.

**semantic memory**. A type of declarative memory (the other is episodic memory). Includes facts, names and language information. The result of our meaning extraction process.

**sensorimotor stage**. Piaget's first stage of cognitive development. Infants are learning to process sensory inputs and perform motor functions. No thinking is occurring (probably not true).

**sensory memory** (sensory register or sensory store). The shortest forms of memory. Inputs are temporarily stored in a buffer or register preceding being processed in working memory. Iconic memory (vision) and echoic memory (hearing) are the best well defined. But smell, taste, and touch may have their own stores.

**sentence completion**. Based on the word association studies of Mary Calkins. A tool for creativity, brainstorming and initiating conversations.

**sequential models**. Helpful for showing how one step leads to another.

**serial interleaving**. Study A, then B, then C, then A, B, C…

**serial movements**. Sequences of discrete movements. Includes serving a tennis ball (toss ball up, swing racket, follow-through, etc.).

**serial position effect**. In long lists of words, when asked to remember them in order, we remember the first of the list best, the end next best and the middle least well.

**serial recall**. Retrieve items in the order presented.

**sham-feeding**. Experimental method of Pavlov, used to study digestion. Food is supplied thru a tube connected to the stomach, bypassing smell, texture and taste cues. Satiety is slower; animals on sham-feeding tend to overeat.

**shaping**. Using continuous reinforcement to reward successive approximations of a desired behavior.

**sheltered workshops**. Also known as work centers. Organizations who are licensed or authorized to employ mentally disabled workers, usually paying sub-minimum wages.

**short-term memory**. Also called working memory. Temporary storage of items or chunks of items. Capacity is ~7 items or chunks (plus or minus 2)

**shuttle box**. An enclosure with a short net or wall separating it into two parts. When a shock is applied on one side, the animal shuttles (jumps over) to the other side of the box.

**side effects**. Unintended consequences. Punishment is a good example of behaviors with bad consequence (angry, aggression and modeling lack of control).

**sidetracking method**. One of Guthrie's ways to break habits. Distraction.

**sign tracking** (auto-shaping). A phenomenon in classical conditioning which appears to involve operant conditioning. Two stimuli are paired with no regard to the animal behavior. A key is lit before food appears (for example). When the food appears, the pigeon (our subject) orients to the food and eats it. Over time, the pigeon orients to the key when it lights up (looks at, turns toward it, pecks at it as if it was food). Auto-shaping is not easily explained by Skinner's model.

**similar dimensions**. We remember directions is a two-stage process. We learn the dimension and then the sub-action. When we learn we are to turn a switch up or down, we never try to flip it left or right, but we often forget it up or down is the correct response.

**similarity**. One of Aristotle's laws of association. We remember things that are similar to each other. A type of chunking.

**Simon, Herbert**. A major force in psychology, economics, decision-making, computer science and problem solving. Bounded rationality.

**Simonides of Ceos**. Famous poet and memory expert in ancient Greece. Described as wise, miserly, inventive and colorful. Story has it that at a tragedy, he was able to identify bodies by where they were seated when the roof collapsed. Used the method of loci.

**simple skills**. Can be continuous or discrete. Require very little thought or energy. Includes flipping a light switch, spinning a top, twirling a Hula-Hoop and pushing a doorbell.

**single subject designs** (N=1). One subject is studied at a time.

**single-blind study**. The subjects don't know which experimental group they are in (single blind). The people who administer or run the experiment don't know who is in which experimental group (double blind). The people who analyze the results don't know what the study is trying to prove (triple blind).

**six steps of problem solving**. Tangen's model of questions for solving problems: where am I now, where do I want to be, how do I get from here to there, will this work, try it out, repeat. Also presented as: now, want, how, this, try, now.

**sketch cognitive map**. Uses landmarks for navigation (drive until you see a big tree).

**Skinner, Burrhus Frederic** (1904-1990). Skinner's work was both atheoretical and inductive. He expanded Thorndike's law of effect to an entire system of reinforcement. He emphasized what happens after a response. Not S-R, but S-R-C (stimulus-response-consequence), Conceding that there are too many stimuli to categorize, Skinner focused on the response and its consequence.

With positive reinforcers there is an increase in behavior. The likelihood of the behavior occurring again is higher. Positive punishment decreases behavior temporarily (as long as the punisher is present). Only extinction (the continued absence of a reward) decreases behavior permanently (e.g., if they stop paying you, you don't go to work).

Negative reinforcement (the removal of something bad) increases the likelihood of behavior and negative punishment (the removal of something good) temporarily decreases it.

Basing his findings on animal research (mostly rats and pigeons), Skinner identified five schedules of reinforcement: continuous reinforcement (a reward is given each time), fixed interval (FI), fixed ratio (FR), variable interval (VI) and variable ratio (VR). Continuous reinforcement is used to shape (refine) a behavior. Every time the subject performs the desired behavior, it is rewarded. Continuous reinforcement leads to quick learning and (after the reinforcement is stopped) quick descent.

In an attempt to apply his research to practical problems, Skinner adapted his operant conditioning chamber (he hated the popular title of "Skinner box") to child rearing. His "Baby Tender" crib was an air conditioned glass box which he used for his own daughter for two and a half years. Although commercially available, it was not a popular success.

Skinner's also originated programmed instruction. Using a teaching machine (or books with small quizzes which lead to different material), small bits of information are presented in an ordered sequence. Each frame or bit of information must be learned before one is allowed to proceed to the next section. Proceeding to the next section is thought to be rewarding.

**small number of assumptions**. One of Tangen's CUSSIT criteria for testing a theory. A theory with a few assumptions is better than a theory with a lot of assumptions.

**social intelligence**. Knowledge about how to interact with people. Requires tact and flexibility.

**social learning theory**. Later called social cognitive theory. A series of theorists who believe that personality is not set but learned from social interaction.

**social psychology**. The study of why people do what they do in normal situations. Includes predictable irrationality and buying decisions.

**sounds like**. When you can't remember something, asking yourself what the word sounds like. A type of lexical retrieval.

**source amnesia**. The tendency for us to remember what we read or heard but not encode who said it or where we heard it.

**source monitoring**. Tracking where we got a piece of information. Humans are very poor at source monitoring. We are meaning extractors.

**sparse encoding**. Complex images and situations are stored in memory as guidelines, fragments or outlines. We store extracted meanings and overall impressions.

**spatial memory**. Recall of location information. Used to run mazes or find your way across town. Requires the integration of information from the hippocampus, posterior parietal lobe and the prefrontal cortex. Involved in creating and using cognitive maps.

**spatial reasoning**. The ability to visualize and mentally manipulate 2- and 3-dimensional objects (twisting them, flipping them, and predicting which side will appear.

**speeded tests**. Lots of easy questions but with limited time to answer them.

**split-brain people**. To stop rebounding seizures, epileptic has corpus callosum surgically severed. The hemispheres operate more independently, though linked by many other neural crossings. Have initial difficulty coordinating hand-eye combinations.

**spontaneous recovery**. The tendency for responses to return to higher levels of frequency after extinction. Occurs in both classical and operant conditioning.

**spotlight effect**. The cognitive bias that people notice you more than they actually do.

**spread of effect**. For Pavlov, the tendency for stimuli similar to the conditioned stimulus to produce a conditioned response caused by adjacent neurons being impacted by the conditioning.

**S-R**. Stimulus-response. The basic premise of classical conditioning is that a stimulus elicits a response.

**stamped in.** Before models of neural circuit reiteration, Thorndike proposed that problem solving is not insight but trial and error until the correct response is discovered; the impact of the positive consequence which follows that discovery (law of effect) makes a permanent relationship (stamps in) between problem and solution.

**stamped out**. For Thorndike, learning is permanent unless erased by negative consequences after the response.

**state variables**. A term introduced by Skinner to indicate initial, antecedent conditions before stimulation begins.

**state-dependent learning**. Internal states (mood, pain, etc.) impact our ability to learn and remember. When you are happy, you remember happy things. When you are sad, you remember sad things. It is easier to remember when internal states match between learning and retrieval.

**status-quo bias**. Tendency to be reluctant to change. Stay with routines.

**stereotypes**. Cognitive filters which we use to pre-categorize people, objects and environments. Culturally learned ideas which are fixed, oversimplified and difficult to change.

**stimulus generalization**. The tendency for stimuli similar to the conditioned stimulus to produce a conditioned response.

**store recipes**. We don't store exact copies of an experience, we store its parts. We extract meaning from a scene and discard the rest. We store recipes, not entire meals.

**storyboard**. A graphic way to organize and sequence stories and presentations. Widely used in the production of animations, movies and video games. Originally developed in the 1930s by Walt Disney.

**straight-run maze**. A maze with no twists or turns. Used to explain the conflicts studied by Dollard & Miller.

**stress**. Generalized, nonspecific response to perceived threats. Stress levels can impact learning or performance.

**string on your finger**. A physical reminder. Helps alert you that something needs to be remembered but doesn't help indicate what it is that needs to be recalled.

**Stroop effect**. Can't say color of word; say the word. Evidence of top-down processing.

**structural overview**. A summary, usually visual, of what is or will be learned in a lesson. Can be used as an introduction, a review or both.

**study skills**. A series of tasks and practices used by good students. The list usually includes a designated study space, a consistent environment, note taking techniques and mnemonic strategies.

**stupidity-misery syndrome**. For Dollard and Miller, neurosis is a combination of stupidity (not knowing the label of how you feel) and misery (can effectively discriminate).

**subvocalized speech**. For Watson, thinking is the behavior of talking to oneself at inaudible (subvocalized) levels of sound.

**successive approximations**. A common description of shaping. Rewards are given for behaviors that are closer to the desired behavior. At first, rewards are given for less than perfect performance. Gradually, the criteria is increased.

**summarizes facts**. One of Tangen's CUSSIT criteria for testing a theory. A theory which summarizes more facts is better than a theory which summarizes less facts.

**superstitious behavior**. Behaviors which are inadvertently rewarded.

**suppressed background**. When perceiving an object, the mind deemphasizes the background, making it less noticeable. At the same time, the foreground in highlighted, making the distinction even more obvious.

**switch tasks**. A study technique. Change to studying a different topic as proactive interference builds up. Switch on the basis of time (every 15-20 minutes) or fatigue (focus is shifting) or flow (flow is an indication you've mastered the material).

**systematic desensitization**. A behavior therapy developed by Wolpe, particularly helpful for phobias. A hierarchy of fear stimuli is created. The patient is taught systematic relaxation. A stimulus from the hierarchy is presented or imagined while the patient remains relaxed. Any anxiety stops the presentation and a stimulus lower in the hierarchy is presented. Based on the assumption that fear and relaxation are incompatible responses.

**T**

**tactile encoding**. Encoding the texture and physical characteristics of an object.

**talent**. A special aptitude or ability. Usually thought of as a built-in or biologically determined entity. Includes creative, athletic and musical talent. Less a predictor of success than perseverance.

**Tangen's two great principles of human behavior**. Tangen's conclusion that (a) people have a tremendous capacity to change, and (b) they usually don't change.

**target behaviors**. Specific things you can do to maintain a target skill. Includes keeping your eye on the ball,

**target contexts**. Environments in which you perform a skill or task. Vary in friendliness, competitiveness, duration and intensity.

**target skills**. In skill building, the broad goals for a given task. In tennis, for example, a target skill might be keeping the ball in play.

**target stick** (follow stick). Used to train animals to walk and stand quietly. Particularly valuable in horse training. The animal is rewarded for touching its nose to the stick. The stick is gradually moved to different positions over the course of several trials. Once the nose-to-target behavior is well established, the stick and be used to walk a horse up a rank, etc.

**task analysis**. A detail description of how a task is done. The task is broken down into its smallest steps. The report can be used to instruct someone else in how to perform the task.

**taste aversion**. Also called conditioned taste aversion. An aversion formed by classical conditioning, often in a single trial. You eat something spoiled or toxic, usually an unusual food. You become nauseated and avoid the food in the future. You might also avoid the restaurant and the entire style of cooking.

**teach someone**. A technique to improve encoding. When you are confident you understand a concept, explain it to someone else. Teaching others shows hole in our reasoning.

**teaching machine**. Originally, a mechanical device used to present small amounts of information to students. Based on Skinner's programmed learning approach. Now instructional programs are run on computers, tablets or are web-based.

**technical mnemonics**. Memory techniques that don't come naturally to us but can be learned. The most helpful are method of loci (visualizing a concept at each point along a journey) and backward chaining (adding links to the front of a chain).

**test yourself**. A study technique. Before you take a test prepared by someone else, make up test questions and see how you would answer them.

**testable hypotheses**. One of Tangen's CUSSIT criteria for testing a theory. A theory with testable hypotheses is better than a theory without testable hypotheses.

**thinning**. Giving less reward for the same amount of work.

**Thorndike, Edward Lee** (1874-1949). A student of William James, Thorndike proposed that S-R bonds are stamped in and remain in effect until stamped out by a new connection. He studied the puzzle-solving abilities of cats and dogs in puzzle-boxes.

Thorndike's contention was that learning is the process of creating S-R connections ("bonds"). According to him, learning is not insight but trial and error attempts to find the correct response. Once the correct response is discovered it is "stamped in."

In contrast to the belief that a human mind should be trained (with good literature, etc.), Thorndike proposed three laws of learning: readiness, exercise and effect. In place of the trained mind approach to education, Thorndike advocated the "transfer of training." According to his theory, learning new tasks is related to how similar they are to previously learned tasks. That is, transfer depends on how many identical elements are held in common.

Similarly, Thorndike's definition of intelligence is the amount of transfer capacity. He identified three types of intelligence: abstract, social and mechanical. There is no general mental ability as far as Thorndike was concerned.

**thoughts**. For Dollard and Miller, thoughts are cue-producing responses in the brain.

**three things you can learn**. Tangen's model of learning that suggests you can only learn facts, concepts and behaviors.

**threshold method**. For Guthrie, the gradual increase of stimulus strength without producing unwanted responses (e.g., gradually entering a pool to conquer fear of water).

**time out**. A poplar form of negative punishment.

**time-gap**. Arrive at home but with no conscious recollection having driven there. Similar to highway hypnosis.

**tip of tongue phenomenon**. The common experience (about once per week) of not being able to find the right word.

**token economy**. Based on Skinner's reinforcement theory. Used in schools, prisons and families. Tokens (poker chips, points, etc.) are earned by doing targeted behaviors.

**Tolman, Edward** (1886-1959). Best known for his purposive behaviorism. Tolman introduced the intervening variable as a description of indirect influence. An intervening variable is caught in-between two other variables.

**top-down processing**. Perceptual processing theory that the brain actively looks ahead to identify incoming information. A preview scan on incoming information. Used for categorizing friend-foe, focusing attention, and identifying the input as words or music. The opposite of bottom-up processing (perception & sensation).

**total time hypothesis**. Ebbinghaus proposal that recall in linearly related to how much time you spent on it.

**Tower of Hanoi**. A mental puzzle or game, with posts and discs. The discs have to be moved one at a time, and a larger one can never be on top of a smaller one. Success is defined as the smallest number of turns. With 3 poles (number of discs doesn't matter), it is a closed environment (well-defined problem). An algorithm can solve the puzzle. With more than 3 poles, it is an open environment (ill-defined problem). No algorithm can solve the problem.

**trace conditioning**. Classical conditioning with to overlap between the CS and the UCS presentation. More difficult to learn than forward conditioning.

**trace decay theory**. A theory of forgetting that proposes forgetting is the automatic fading (decay) of memory traces (engrams). Replaced by interference theories.

**track, try** & reward strategy. A three-stage strategy for behavior change. First, tracking alone is tried. Then, tracking a behavior is tracked while you try to change. Finally, the target behavior is tracked and rewarded. Shows the relative influence of rewards. Often tracking is enough to change a behavior.

**tracking**. Charting or counting the number of times a target behavior occurs. The first step to changing a behavior.

**trained mind**. Attributed to Locke, the best approach to learning is thought to be teaching people to think. Typically, this approach emphasizes mathematics or literature classes, and deemphasizes practical or domain-specific knowledge.

**transfer of training**. For Thorndike, learning new tasks is related to how similar they are to previously learned tasks. The ability to transfer is based on the amount of identical elements between the two tasks.

**translation schemes**. A technical mnemonic used to remember numbers. An adaptation of the number-shape peg system. Numbers are converted into words, where digits (0 through 9) are consonants and vowels don't count. 1 = t (one vertical stroke), 2 = n (two lines), and 3 = m (3 vertical lines). Converts 13 into tim or tom or team (your coice).

**trial and error learning**. For Thorndike, learning is not insight, but a process of trying all alternatives until a successful response is found. Try all possible combinations

**triarchic theory of successful intelligence**. Robert Sternberg's 3-factor theory: metacognition (executive processing), performance (LTM, doing) and knowledge-acquisition (choosing relevant information).

**triggers**. Stimuli. The term in used rather haphazardly to describe any cue that initiates a thought, behavior, sequence or emotional reaction.

**triple-blind study**. The subjects don't know which experimental group they are in (single blind). The people who administer or run the experiment don't know who is in which experimental group (double blind). The people who analyze the results don't know what the study is trying to prove (triple blind).

**Tulving, Endel**. Canadian psychologist, best known for his encoding specificity principle. Performance is best when it occurs under the same conditions it was learned. The more similar the match, the better the performance.

**two as a swan**. A technical mnemonic for remembering numbers. Both a 2 and a swan have curved necks.

**two-factor theory of intelligence**. Raymond Cattell's distinction between fluid and crystalized intelligence. Fluid intelligence is innate and unchangeable. Crystalized intelligence is learned and impacted by one's culture.

**two-fer**. In dog training, requiring two responses for a treat. Increasing the shaping criterion.

# U

**unconditioned response** (UCR). Reflexive response; requires no learning (conditioning). In Pavlov's studies, the UCR is salivating to food. The natural response to a stimulus before conditioning (e.g., salivating at food).

**unconditioned stimulus** (UCS). Stimulus that triggers (elicits) a reflexive response. In Pavlov's studies, the UCS was the food. The natural stimulus which produces natural responses (e.g. sight or smell of food).

**unidirectional bonds**. In paired associates, bonds between words are formed in one direction. A good practice is to learn flash cards in both cue-definition and definition-cue orientations.

**unlabeled conflicts**. For Dollard & Miller, labeling conflicts breaks their power; think Rumpelstiltskin.

**unresolved conflicts**. It sounds bad but people can disagree on things and still happily live together. Most people in long-term relationships report long-standing unresolved conflicts.

**useful**. One of Tangen's CUSSIT criteria for testing a theory. Vague useful theories are better than clear useless theories.

# V

**variable interval** (VI). Reinforcer is given inconsistently but on average after N minutes. Produces behavior that is resistant to extinction. Don't know when fish will bite or bus will come. One of Skinner's schedules of reinforcement; given for a correct response after a varying period of time.

**variable ratio** (VR). Reinforcer is given inconsistently but on average after every Nth response. Produces behavior that is very resistant to extinction. Don't know how many time have to play for slot machine to pay off. One of Skinner's schedules of reinforcement; given for a correct response after a varying number of correct responses.

**variables**. In general, there are four main types of variables. Dependent variables are outcome variables, and depend on what a subject does. In contrast, independent variables are independent of the subjects. Independent variables are manipulated by the experimenter and often are hidden from the subject. Tolman introduced the concept of intervening variables; it was used as a description of indirect influence. An intervening variable is caught in-between two other variables. State variables (a term introduced by Skinner) indicate initial, antecedent conditions before stimulation begins.

**vector-based cognitive map**. One of two types of cognitive maps. Vector-based (also called grid-based) maps use coordinates and headings. In contrast, sketch maps use landmarks.

**verbal intelligence**. Also called semantic intelligence or book learning. Shows ability to use and understand language and factual information.

**verbal reports**. In addition to behavioral observation (watching what people do), psychology uses self-reports (what people say they do).

**verification**. Putting an idea into practice; testing that it solves the problem. One of four stage of creativity: preparation, incubation, illumination and verification.

**vicarious learning**. For Bandura, being able to learn by watching someone else. Modeling.

**vicarious punishment**. Watching someone else being punished lowers the likelihood of a behavior occurring. Tends to make people careful not to get caught.

**vicarious reinforcement**. Watching someone else being rewards increases the likelihood of a behavior occurring. If others can make it rich, we can too.

**visual encoding**. Meaning is extracted from images and converted into neural patterns.

**visualization**. Creating and using a mental image.

**visuo-spatial sketchpad**. Part of Baddeley's working memory model.

**vividness**. Vivid images are easier to remember than dull images. But vividness is less important than the number of presentations, and the interactivity of mental images.

**voluntary behavior**. What you choose to do.

**von Restorff Effect**. A type of primary distinctiveness. A word of a different font or color in the middle of list makes the whole list easier to remember.

**Vygotsky, Lev**. A Russian psychologist and advocate of active learning. Best known for his "zone of proximal distance."

# W

**waiting room experiment**. Can refer to many studies but often is used to describe the 1981 study of incidental learning by Brewer & Treyens. Subjects waited in room for less than a minute and were then asked to list the objects in the room. Shows evidence of schemas being using in recall.

**War of the Ghosts**. The American folk tale Bartlett used on his British students to test their schema formation. Students corrupted the story to fit into their schema of life.

**warm up trials**. Although implicit memory drops off rather steadily, performance rebounds quick with a few trials. It is as if the brain is a vacuum tube system that needs time for the mechanism to be ready to perform. If you haven't ridden a bicycle for a long time, a few times around the black will bring back most of your performance capability.

**Watson, John Broadus** (1878-1958). Describes the mind as a mystery box (black box). Behavior is the result of brain connections (S-R bonds). Ignoring high mental processes altogether, Watson explained all behavior in terms of stimulus-response. Although he initially allowed for three innate emotions (fear, rage and love), Watson generally denied the influence of heredity on behavior. He helped direct psychology's attention away from speculative theories to experimental observations. From white rats in mazes to "Little Albert," Watson emphasized S-R conditioning. In an attempt to apply behaviorism to practical problems, Watson proposed "experimental ethics," a classical conditioning rehabilitation program for inmates.

**wax tablet**. Ancient view of memory. Memory is not permanent (carved in stone) but mostly permanent and somewhat changeable (like a wax impression).

**well-defined problems** (well-structured). Problems with clear parameters, such as chess, checkers and searching a database. The 3-pole version, but not the 4-pole version, of the Tower of Hanoi problem.

**white rat psychologist**. A term for John Watson, who did many experiments using rats.

**Williams, Ted**. A professional baseball player often referred to as the greatest hitter who ever lived. He achieved his ability through relentless practice, and is used as an example of how practice improves performance.

**withdrawal**. Symptoms from discontinuing a drug. Caused by drug tolerance.

**within list associations**. Ebbinghaus showed that associated words within a list make the list easier to remember. If "cow" and "moo" are in the list, the normal association between them makes them easier to remember. Adjacent associations (cow and moo next to each other) are the strongest word associations.

**word association**. Words connected by shape, sound, adjacency on a list are easier to remember than words that have no associations.

**word lists**. First studied by Ebbinghaus. Lists of words are used to show the limits and processes of memory. Short lists are easy. Long lists are harder and have a specific pattern (the beginning of the list is easier to remember than the end, and the middle of list is least well remembered. Learning lists requires repetition.

**word pairs**. Also called word associations. The connections between words are uni-directional. River-bank is not the same as bank-river.

**word-completion items**. An application of word-associations. Therapists and research use this task (finish the rest of the word) to indicate conflict or to test memory.

**work**. In cognitive terms, a task which requires conscious use of mental processes.

**workflow**. In general, a way to solve a problem. A pattern of activities or a sequence of operations. A collective of the steps it takes to complete a task. Mailing a letter is composed of writing the letter, getting someone else to read it, re-editing, printing, signing, putting in an envelope, licking the seal, adding postage, etc.

**working memory**. Also called short-term. Temporary storage of items or chunks of items. System that holds multiple segments temporarily for immediate attention. Holds ~7 items or chunks. Stays available with rehearsal. Things currently focused on, keep active with rehearsal. Baddeley's working memory model includes a phonological loop, episodic buffer, and a visuo-spatial sketchpad.

**working problems backwards**. Unless constrained by the rules, many problems (such as mazes) are easier to solve backwards. Start at the goal and backtrack.

**worldview**. General attitude and conceptual framework of how the world works and how you fit in it. An antecedent to learning.

**write it down**. The advice of memory experts. Although technical mnemonics can be used, for most daily situations it is far easier to write things down.

**writer's cramp**. Signals in the motor cortex get confused from doing a task too long. Shows there are limits to how long to practice in a single session. Also appears when practicing the guitar, violin or other instrument requiring fine motor movements.

**Wundt, Wilhelm**. Founder of experimental psychology. Theories of will, consciousness and emotion. Learning was not a major concern of early psychologists. The focus was on perception.

LEARN VOCABULARY: LEARNING

# Y

**Ye & Salvendy**. Studied expert and novice computer programmers. Experts knew more (better concrete knowledge) and were better at high levels of abstraction.

# Z

**Zeigarnik Effect**. Named for Bluma Zeigarnik. Incomplete tasks are easier to remember than completed tasks. You can remember the plot when you are reading a chapter a day. But finish the book and the whole plot is less clear.

# PUTTING IT ALL TOGETHER

We've covered a great deal of material. You now know a great deal about the psychology of learning. We covered terms from classical conditioning, habits, operant conditioning, skills, schema, scripts, expectations, and cognitive bias.

You might still have some questions or things you're not sure about. I have a website devoted to learning. Just go to www.psychlearning.com. There are posts, lectures, videos, notes, quizzes and everything else I could think to add. If you can't find what you want, let me know and I'll look into providing it for you.

# ABOUT THE AUTHOR

I have studied psychology most of my life. After earning B.A in psychology, I earned an M.S. in counseling psychology, including all the course work for a masters in experimental psychology. After working a few years, I earned a PhD in a combination of cognition, measurement, education and psychology. I also did internships in counseling and family therapy.

I am a fanatic about teaching. It is my hobby, my love and my calling. I work hard at making complex things seem simple, or at least understandable. Writing is just another way of teaching.

Of course, you get to decide how successful I have been at my job. Feel free to send me your thoughts and comments. If you have positive things to say, email me: ken@kentangen.com. If you have negative things to say, call your mother.

# BONUS

## Free Course

I've created a free 5-day email course on breaking habits. Go to: www.kentangen.com/breaking and sign up.

www.ingramcontent.com/pod-product-compliance
Lightning Source LLC
Chambersburg PA
CBHW070952040426
42443CB00007B/470